DOUBLE TAP

Social Media Marketing 101 for Musicians

Written by Kelly Samuel, Professor of Social Media at Fanshawe College

3rd edition, September 2022.

Introduction to Social Media Marketing 101 4

Marketing 101 8

Brand Alignment 11

Brand Tone Exercise 22

Brand Voice Exercise 29

Brand Tone & Voice Guideline 37

Determine an Aesthetic Strategy 40

Social Media Strategy 50

Social Media Tools for Artists 55

How to create a content strategy 61

Community Pillars 64

Optimizing Instagram Stories 76

How to Increase Ticket Attendance for Events Through Social Media - Organic 78

How to Increase Ticket Attendance for Events Through Social Media – Paid 83

Exploring Content Variations 86

Interaction Online / Offline (Networking through Social) 94

Influencer Marketing & Product Placement 97

Cool Instagram Features to Play With 108

How to Increase Instagram Engagement 112

Hashtag Research 115

Checklist for Going Live 121

Video Strategy 124

Viral Marketing Techniques 128

Marketing Merch Online 133
Optimizing Your Tour Online 140
Promoting through Radio/Social 143
Howdy, you've reached the end.. 150

Introduction to Social Media Marketing 101

If you're reading this, I need you to type this into your computer right now. Don't think, just do it. Now have this playing while you read the rest of this.

https://www.youtube.com/watch?v=rRPQs_kM_nw

Note that this 23 million views at the time that I'm writing this. Yes, this video is a cow dancing for 10 hours straight.

I'm making you listen to this for two key reasons. First, if this link is broken, so is the rest of this book. Social media evolves faster than any other marketing stream on the planet. If you're reading an old version of this book, you need to ditch this copy and purchase the newest version. Instagram and Facebook can sometimes roll out multiple updates a week - there is no possible way for you to compete in this space with outdated information. TikTok has made Instagram panic-update almost weekly. There are plenty of opportunities to save money in the music industry (and believe me, I get it), but this is not one of them. Buy the newest version of this book so we're all on the same page in 2022.

Second, I'm not going to tell you. You can flip ahead to the end if you really want to, but it'll make more sense as we go along.

If you have it playing, you're probably super angry at me right now and that's right where I'd like ya. Here's a little about me.

I'm a social media expert with more than 13 years of experience in this very very very new field. I participated in Facebook's launch into monetization in 2007 as a small business owner, where 100% of my business came through organic or paid social media. I am a Canadian born and raised content creator, having amassed a total of around 10K organic followers on Instagram. I have contributed a dozen articles to Forbes.com about social media marketing, digital trends, and digital marketing tips for other agency members. Notably, I have also been featured by Global News in an interview about social media ethics, The Globe and Mail on Instagram, and have delivered seminars on digital marketing internationally.

I founded two different marketing agencies in Toronto ON. Before I left the first one, social media management accounted for more than half of total agency revenue after a short 5 year period. I left and went on to found Let's Snack Toronto, a social media agency for food and beverage brands. I create strategy, hire, train and manage the team, and come up with newer ways of executing social media management for brands, businesses, and key figures.

Prior to Let's Snack Toronto, I was a content creator with popular radio station 881.FM Indie88, contributing nearly 100 articles on pop-culture and relevant events for their social channels. Prior to this, I was the Director of Marketing at 94.9 CHRW Radio at Western University.

When I was in University, I joined an indie-pop band called Olivia and the Creepy Crawlies. I was their backing-vocalist, involuntary glockenspiel player, acoustic guitar player (in the later years), but most notably social media manager. Like you, I've slept on hardwood floors, I've played amazing shows to empty rooms, and I've faced the challenge of creating exposure and sales for a new act.

I've played shows where other acts had purchased followers on Instagram or Facebook, drew 0 people out to a show but (somehow) secured a guarantee based on fake Facebook likes. I've played shows where the headlining act didn't advertise the show in favour of another local gig around the same time. I've played shows where we've sold out venues. I've also played shows where despite good ticket sales, no one showed up. We toured on and off for 5 years. I missed every family and social obligation you can think of - I was fully immersed in this space. Then there was a time of overlap where I worked 40 hours a week at the agency, and another 40 hours a week with the band. My experience and background are highly integral to this book.

This book is a compilation of my trials, failures, insights and marketing experience for artists and bands. I hope it helps you get started.

Marketing 101

Social media is one element of marketing. Marketing includes a bunch of different streams including SEO, print, design, PR, experiential, and more. The gist behind this is that we're trying to sell a product or a service by selling an idea. Specifically, we're trying to sell the idea of you as an artist, so we can then sell specific items like albums and merch.

The goal is to sell a specific lifestyle or a dream or a feeling. Marketing is a runaround way of trying to sell people happiness by associating specific moments in time with a tangible product or service. Some might purchase a spa day because you want to feel relaxed. Some might buy champagne because it makes them feel excited and celebratory. Some might buy into an artist because it makes them feel closer to youth, happiness, joy, or some other element of connectedness.

So to start, how many times do you think it takes for someone to see something before they recognize it?

7 times. It takes on average 7 times for something visual to stick in the minds of the average consumer.

This means that as a musician or an artist, we need to communicate who we are at least 7 times before we can start to create brand awareness.

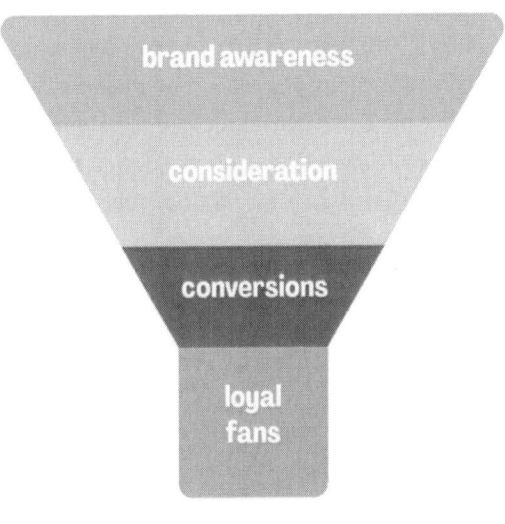

Le Purchase Funnel

Brand awareness is the very opening of the purchase funnel. First people must know who you are, and once they know who you are, you can start to move them into the "consideration" part of the funnel. This translates to getting someone to engage with your social media content, enter in your contests, react in polls, or sign up for your mailing list. Consideration features often means a fan is willing to invest their time, but not their money yet.

Once we get to the conversion part of the funnel it means that they know who you are, they're interested in what you represent and the music you make, and they're ready to spend money. These are the folks that will show up to buy a ticket to a show, an EP or album, or merch.

Loyal fans are ideally where we want to be - we want to use social media as a tool to amass your own group of loyal and dedicated ambassadors, ready to rep you at every given opportunity. This is what you're going to learn through this short primer - use this as a guide, follow the steps, and ask questions wherever you can.

Brand Alignment

Let's start with your act. What feelings, ideas, or dreams are we trying to sell?

If this exercise proves difficult, think to your favourite artists and bands. What do you experience when you listen to your favourite album of favourite song right now?

Some extremely common (and successful) themes in mainstream music are youth, beauty, and sex.

Some successful feelings that permeate a lot of alternative music are nostalgia, sadness, anger, or betrayal.

To turn this into an idea, you'll want to flesh it out to something like this:

Artist: Lana Del Rey

Recurring themes & feelings: America, capitalism, romance, vanity, death, longing, desperation, nostalgia, loneliness, apathy

The way that this gets communicated is through persona, or brand alignment. Every piece of Lana Del Rey's music is doused with added personality or baggage – songs aren't standalone lore. They are a story, told by a young, lonely girl in retro America, being sold a dream of capitalism, vanity and romance.

Even before you name your act or your band, you should talk about this. Who are you and what ideas, dreams or feelings are you trying to sell?

Pick a Name

After you've determined what vibe you're going for (see Brand Alignment Chapter), you'll want to pick a name that matches your tone. Are you aiming to make people feel nostalgic? Moody? Sad? Elated? Excited? Inspired? What are some common themes you think tie into the emotions you've picked?

You want to make sure that it's specific, simple, and memorable. Try to find inspiration in your muse for writing, and avoid cliché names that are about music itself. Before you get too sold on anything, google it. Make sure no one else is currently operating under that moniker, or it could be very costly to change names later down the road.

After you google it, try using https://www.namecheckr.com/ to see if it's taken across .com, Instagram, tiktok, twitter, and Facebook. This is a really quick and simple tool to identify what's available across the board. You'll want to make sure it's the same handle across all channels, and short enough to fit both on social media and on stickers or business cards. If it's on the longer side, try out different acronyms or short forms — because if you don't, someone else will, and what sticks may not be something you like. HOTD (House of The Dragon) comes to mind.

Next, think about your childhood bully and all the ways your name could be misconstrued. Is there a hidden double entendre? Does it make a funny acronym, or look like something else when it's written? Be your own bully, check for unintentional spelling or phrasing.

If you're going to use satiric misspelling of some kind, try to make it have a point. AKA Chvrches or any other variance of

13

this. It will get annoying to spelling it out every time you meet a new fan, and it makes it harder for fans to find you.

Stuck on where to go next, or starting a band and can't agree on genre or themes? Try using a generator like below, or some other fun name generators

- https://www.name-generator.org.uk/band-name/
- Your Mom's maiden name, and the last thing you went to the hospital for
- The last strong feeling you had, and the last place you travelled to
- The last thing you ate, and the first thing you saw this morning
- Your siblings middle name, and your favourite physical attribute
- An adjective to describe the last object you touched, and the name of your hometown

Define Your Roles

Once you have your name, you need to establish who does what without your team. As musicians, you will learn to have several hats – some of you will be much better copywriters than others, some of you may be better with design or strategy. Whatever it is, make sure these roles are equally divvied up, as marketing your music can be just as much work as creating it.

    a. Strategist - this is the person who comes up with the ideas, leads brainstorming sessions, and adds the initial concepts into the content calendar. This is the "big ideas" person. They are constantly looking for better and more creative ways of coming across, and should be actively keeping up with other brands/bands/artists that are in your sphere, to make sure you're staying relevant.

    b. Copywriter - this is the person whose caption game is on point. They have to be able to come up with the copy, or captions, for your content calendar. They are also the leading person developing your band bio, with the help of the Social Media Manager, the Editor, and the Strategist. The copywriter ensures that your brand tone is homogenous.

    c. Editor - this is the person who has excellent grammar, punctuation, and spelling. This person is able to think critically and contextually about the calendar, and should be able to catch any flaws, mistakes, or possible issues before the calendar goes out. If there's a potential PR crisis (for example, posting something that could be construed as racist or sexist or accidentally off-putting), the Editor will be able to point it out.

d. Content creator/curator - This is the person who takes the photos/videos, or finds photos from stock photo websites. This person has an excellent eye for visual aesthetics, and knows what looks good across the board. They can tell if an image doesn't fit the rest of the images, or if something looks too stock or contrived.

e. Social Media Manager - this is the person who manages the social media calendar, and makes sure people are doing their jobs. They are also the person who physically posts to Instagram, as well as uploads the Instagram & Facebook stories. They stay on top of everything, and should be in constant communication with all members of the team. The Social Media Manager should be the last person who approves the content calendar before anything goes out.

f. Community Manager - The person who responds to comments, DMs, and questions. This person has to check all social media accounts daily (at the very minimum once a day, but the best case scenario, multiple times a day). This person should be aware of the brand voice/tone, and should do their best to carry it forward when responding to any kind of communication on behalf of the artist.

Determine Brand Identity & Tone

Now that you've got your basics covered, you'll want to identify what direction you're going to take your socials. This means identifying your branding - your tone, your aesthetic, your creative accompaniment to your content. Not what you're communicating, but your delivery of what you're communicating. This is sometimes the part that comes wicked easy to some people. This is often the hardest part for others. Here's a short guide to developing your brand for your act. This information will answer the question of - what do I actually put up when I have nothing to announce, release, or really say? This forms your fluff content, your everything in between content.

1. **Determine your brand identity**

If you're a solo artist, this part is extremely easy. This could simply be your own identity. But depending on what direction you want to take your work, it may be a completely different identity from yourself. If you're in a band or group, this is significantly tougher. You need to determine, if your group was 1 person, who would they be? See the exercise later in this chapter. Physically List:

- What's their age?
- What's their gender?
- What are their likes/dislikes?

Oftentimes, this person is a middle ground of all members. Whatever you do, make it memorable. Have discernable likes/dislikes and hobbies. You want to be crafting a persona that people can reach out and tangibly relate to. This means being as specific as possible. Take Taylor Swift for example. Her brand voice and her target demographic were the same - 14 year old girls, brought up in middle class suburbia, with no real challenges except for love and angst. She was incredibly successful with her target demographic for a number of reasons marketing wise, but her relatability to her fans was at the very top. They felt that she was inside of her head, telling their own stories. That's what you want to strive for too. If it's easier to do this in reverse, then you can try that too. Who is your target demographic of fans? What do they like and dislike, and how does it tie in to the feelings and themes you're trying to sell?

To further our Lana Del Rey narrative, this might translate as a 13-21 year old female, enjoys weed, has depression, highly intelligent and very lonely, interested in vanity, bit of a loner. Quick to get into a tough spot, poor, mysterious, a good time to party with. Loves Americana, vocab and singing style is Transatlantic.

It sounds a bit much to go through this, but once you can picture what your act would be as a singular person, it becomes obvious how it will relate to your target demographic. What do you want your fans to have in common with your music? Literally write out a list of likes and dislikes, and you'll never have a lack of content to talk about. This process can also make songwriting a bit easier, because you can refresh your pool of muses whenever you feel like it.

2. Determine your brand voice

This is the natural tone that all of your copy will be written in. Is your act sarcastic? Emotional? Witty? Professional? Write out a bunch of defining facets of your tone. Every single piece of social media that goes out, every blog post, every message, every comment, needs to adhere to this. Otherwise it feels inauthentic and super weird.

What are some ways we communicate language through text?

You'll want to set rules for punctuation and emojis. Emojis are a very new language. Set definitive rules on how you engage with it. Do you capitalize words when you start a new sentence? Do you use multiple emojis and use question marks? Is your copy short, poetic, and moody? Younger demographics tend to avoid capitalization and focus on emojis. Older demographics tend to overuse punctuation (think about how many ellipses are in a message from one of your parents). Set out guidelines on how you interact with language. Here are a few ways that the same thing can be communicated with different language.

Wholesome, relatable copy:

Hello Toronto! We're SO grateful and appreciative of all of you for sharing our new album, Mushroom Death Sexy Bummer Party!! Please make sure to buy a ticket to our release show at the Horsehoe Tavern on December 3rd 2021! Thanks!! See you there!!

Abstract, cool copy:

 10.03.2021. Link in bio

Both communicate a similar message, both work, but deciding which direction you go will also decide which kind of fans you'll

19

be favoring communication with. Either direction you go, try to incorporate emojis and a call to action.

Newer ways of communicating language: tone indicators.

One of my students last year (shout out Arthur / Saskatoon!) introduced me to this term, which is a method that clearly lays out tone by using /j (for joking), /g (for genuine) /s (for sarcastic) etc. Apparently this is very popular in the neurodivergent community, as it can be difficult for many who are neurodivergent to read tone. Something to consider for your own copy or voice. Here is a resource that explains this very well :

https://toneindicators.carrd.co/

There is also a communication & accessibility lesson to be learned from the ant uprising of 2020. When the pandemic hit there was a lot of weird stuff that happened – one that stands out to me was the emergence of a Facebook group called "A group where we all pretend to be ants in a colony". It has 1.8 million people in it. The concept was super simple – someone posts something, all users either write D I G or N O M or L I F T or whatever it might be. This tonality of all caps, only actions, no punctuation, no context, and spaces between the letters became a bit of a cultural phenomenon. It was revised once it became apparent that those who are visually impaired utilize software to read aloud, and it couldn't understand the words when there were spaces separating the letters. Sometimes you need to be open to shifting your tone with time as you get more information.

Before you start the exercise, I implore you to think of your music and your artistry as a being and persona separate for yourself. Make it interesting. If it's based off of you, pull out the parts of your personality that shine. Commit fully – if you're picking half measures on every question, you're going to have a watery brand for at the end of it all. Really try to craft something interesting, because the more niche and specific it is, the easier it will be to attract like-minded fans to your music.

Brand Tone Exercise

Brand tone is the lens that conveys emotional inflection. This is conveyed through humour, diction, warmth, etc.

If your band/group/artist was one person, what would be their sense of humour?

◯ Serious

◯ Lighthearted

◯ Teasing

◯ Sarcastic

◯ Sardonic

◯ Slapstick

◯ Self Deprecating

◯ Surreal or absurd

◯ Improv

◯ Witty

◯ Dad Jokes

◯ Topical (Current events or trends)

◯ Dark

◯ Cheeky

Brand Tone Exercise (ii)

If your band/group/artist was one person, how forward would they be?

Select all that apply

◯ Introspective

◯ Passive

◯ Neutral

◯ Assertive

◯ Bold

◯ In Your Face

◯ Cocky

◯ Mysterious

◯ Shy

◯ Coy

Brand Tone Exercise (iii)

If your band/group/artist was one person, what's closest to what your digital speaking style will be?

Select all that apply

- [ ] hey guys 😭 wake up. let's get this bread
- [ ] hey 👋 how r u? let's get this 🍞
- [ ] Hello to each and every one of you! Today is a gorgeous day and we're ready to get started.. who's with me??
- [ ] Howdy! 👋 Let's go!
- [ ] 👋 ☀️ 🫴 🍞

Brand Tone Exercise (iv)

If your band/group/artist was one person, how sincere would they appear to be?

Select all that apply

◯ Down to earth

◯ Honest

◯ Wholesome

◯ Careful

◯ Guarded

◯ Trusting

◯ Sly

◯ Mysterious

◯ Nervous

◯ Cold

Brand Tone Exercise (v)

If your band/group/artist was one person, how excited would they appear to be?

Select all that apply

○ Calm

○ Cool and collected

○ Puppy energy

○ Daring

○ Adventurous

○ Ready for Anything

○ 10 cups of coffee excited

○ Mellow

○ Anxious

○ All Vibes

Brand Tone Exercise (vi)

If your band/group/artist was one person, how sophisticated would they appear to be?

Select all that apply + add your own

◯ Charming

◯ 90s Posh Spice

◯ Pretentious

◯ High Class

◯ Festival camping energy

◯ Glamorous

◯ Extra

◯ Gritty

◯ Broke College Student Status

◯ Vegas residency material

◯ Opera material

Brand Tone Exercise (vii)

If your band/group/artist was one person, how competent would they appear to be?

Select all that apply + add your own

- Highly technical
- Resourceful
- Ditsy
- Hardworking
- Competent but laid back
- A leader
- A good wingman
- "I have people for that"
- Understated
- Simple

Brand Voice Exercise

Brand Voice is your artist's personality. It is unchanging and constant. It is related to your brand tone. If your band/group/artist was one person, what gender would they appear to be?

Select all that apply + add your own

○ Female

○ Male

○ Non-binary

Brand Voice Exercise (ii)

If your band/group/artist was one person, how old would they appear to be?

Select all that apply + add your own

- ◉ Gen A
- ◉ Gen Z
- ◉ Millennial (Gen Y)
- ◉ Gen x
- ◉ Boomer
- ◉ Other

Brand Voice Exercise (iii)

If your band/group/artist was one person, how would they feel about body mods or expression?

Select all that apply + add your own

◯ Tattoos, piercings and other differing varying fashion statements & logos are all welcomed and on brand for us

◯ Non facial tattoos & piercings are welcome. Neutral fashion statements without logos are on brand for us.

◯ We have a strict dress code and it is formal/jazz band

◯ We have a strict dress code and it is floral/cottagecore

◯ We have a strict dress code and it is 70s

◯ We have a strict dress code and it is _____

Brand Voice Exercise (iv)

If your band/group/artist was one person, how big would their social circle be?

Select all that apply + add your own

◯ We know everyone, and everyone knows us

◯ We have a niche amount of followers that follows us for shitposting or memes

◯ We have a main friend group of likeminded individuals

◯ We're the girl at the party that wants to be asked to dance but her hands are way too clammy

◯ We're a lone wolf with a cult following, and we prefer it that way

Brand Voice Exercise (v)

If your band/group/artist was one person, how tidy would they be?

Select all that apply + add your own

◯ Absolutely spotless - OCD

◯ Clean and tidy

◯ Tidy most of the time

◯ Cluttered and we love it

◯ Cluttered and a bit of a hot mess

Brand Voice Exercise (v)

If your band/group/artist was one person, what kind of hobbies would they be into?

Select all that apply + write specifics beside each applicable item.

- ⚪ Hockey (List teams)
- ⚪ Baseball (List teams)
- ⚪ Fitness (What kind?)
- ⚪ Music (List influences or albums)

_____

_____

- ⚪ Art (List artists)
- ⚪ Health
- ⚪ Wellness
- ⚪ Drinking
- ⚪ Soccer
- ⚪ Smoking
- ⚪ Drugs
- ⚪ Reading

- ◉ Writing
- ◉ Yoga
- ◉ Puzzles
- ◉ Travel
- ◉ Spirituality
- ◉ Dancing
- ◉ Astrology
- ◉ Fishing
- ◉ Coding
- ◉ Video Games
- ◉ AI
- ◉ Calligraphy
- ◉ Volunteer Work
- ◉ Theatre
- ◉ Learning Languages
- ◉ Napping
- ◉ Skydiving
- ◉ Cooking
- ◉ TikTok
- ◉ Lazy Sundays
- ◉ Going to the gym

● Museums

Brand Tone & Voice Guideline

Artist name: _____

Social media handles: _____

Brand Voice:
_____
_____
_____
_____
_____
_____
_____
_____

Gender:
_____
_____

Age:
_____
_____

Body Mods / Expression:
_____
_____

How big is their social circle:
_____
_____

Politics or World Events:

_____

_____

How tidy are they?

_____

_____

What kind of hobbies do they have?

_____

_____

_____

_____

_____

Brand Tone

- Humour:
  _____

- Assertiveness:
  _____

- Sincerity:
  _____

- Energy/excitement:
  _____

- Vibe:
  _____

- Competency:
  _____

- Digital Speaking Stye:
  _____

Determine an Aesthetic Strategy

Your aesthetic strategy describes what your accompanying imagery will look like. It should directly relate to your brand alignment, and your themes. Here are some descriptive aesthetics, see if you relate to any of them or if it resonates with your music.

Moody, lo-fi, bright, poppy, polished, goth, macabre, alien, off-putting, monochrome, iridescent, pink, rainbow, 60's, muted, two toned, fluorescent, kaleidoscope, boho, cabaret, bubblegum goth, naturalist, minimalist, black metal, K-pop, VSCO, fantasy, emo, sepia, high contrast, blown out, woodsy, contemporary, grey, dreamy, high school pop, bad bitch, Lolita, yellow, witchy, medieval, post modern, pastel, pointillism, abstract, soft light, claymation, bright white, nautical, natural wood

Unfortunately I can't include a bunch of imagery here (because I'd have to either make it or get publishing rights lol), but try typing in any of the descriptors above into google images or into Pinterest. You need to really look at everything to decide what you like and what you don't like. You can also take inspiration from a band you really like if you like their visual strategy. For visual platforms like Instagram and Facebook this makes lots of sense – and especially for your website. For places like Reels, TikTok or YouTube, this might just mean picking a colour scheme for fonts, and a cool graphic style for titles. You could also pick a "uniform" for your clothing, but it depends on what access to resources you have.

1. Pick a filter or editing style

There are many different ways to do this, the one that will give you the most control is always photoshop. However, as artists, our time should be spent honing our craft, not our design skills, so if you don't have a graphic designer on board, here are some quick apps that can replace a manual edit.

- **Cinemagraph** - this app allows you to create cinemagraphs from videos on your phone. A cinemagraph is a type of video that appears to be a still image, but one part of the image is moving, such as steam coming off of a coffee cup, or the background of an otherwise still image. They're super cool and absolutely under used.

- **Unfold** - this app allows you to create story templates that look sleek, modern and editorial. It may not be the look that you want, but it's a great place to start.

- **VSCO** - this app is a must. There are dozens of free preset filters that you can choose from, and even more that you can purchase. Toss each image into your filter before you post and your grid will always look cohesive, no matter what the subject matter or the camera that you shot it on.

- **Face tune** - this app was popularized because of it's infamous body shaping features, but the reason why it's on this list is actually the whiten and paint features. It's a more simplified version of features that are available on photoshop, which is perfect for subtly incorporating your aesthetic/brand colours into your feed.

Instagram is a very visual platform, but TikTok isn't necessarily, and Reels isn't either. It doesn't hurt to have your content look great on a glance, but it has become less important as content being interesting on an individual level. Pick your aesthetic, and if it helps to pick what tools you'll use for your aesthetic, you can do this part backwards. But first step, find some images or videos that you really like that you'd like to recreate. Once you decide what your aesthetic is, we can get what the content is actually going to be, and how to make it.

How to Create a 9 Grid Using Reels in Photoshop

Reels is (at the time of writing this) an unsaturated feature, and as such it's the best feature to grow using Instagram. If you are OCD like me and ALSO want your feed to look aesthetically pleasing, or just want that extra wow factor, here's what you do.

First have your full image ready to cut into images in Photoshop

Next you're going to turn on rulers by hitting Command R or View> Rulers

Once rulers are on, hit the crop tool. Ensure the aspect ratio is 1:1. For the grid type, select Rule of Thirds if it defaults you to a different grid type.

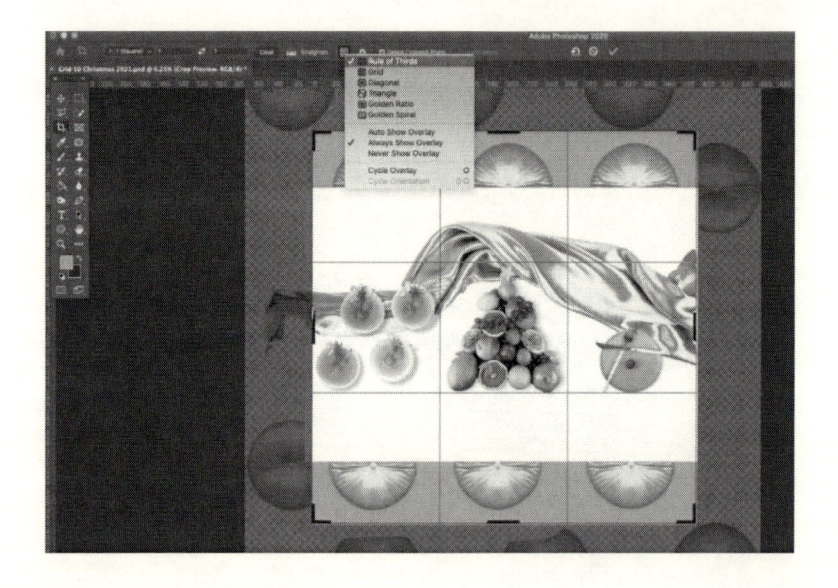

Next, drag your rulers from above and from the left to line up with the 9 grid from the crop tool

Next, you're going to add rules at the halfway point of each image. The center cut is already highlighted by the crop tool, you'll want to eyeball it for the other two OR change the Grid type from Rule of Thirds to Grid to make this easier.

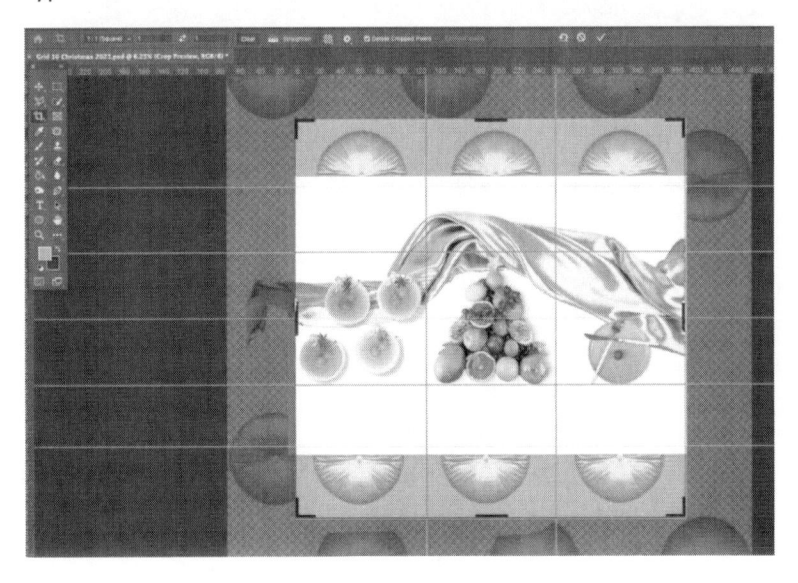

45

Now we're going to change the crop from 1:1 to 9:16. Your screen will look like this.

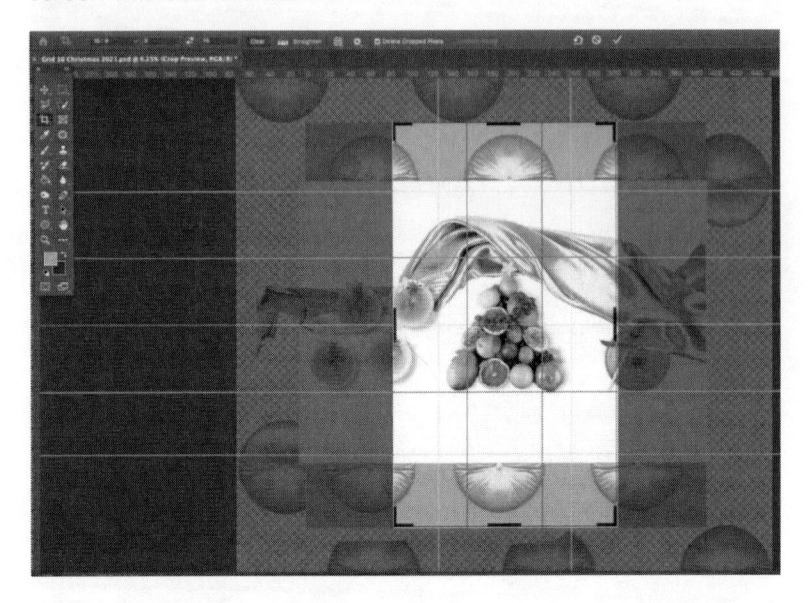

From here you want to drag out the crop so the full width of your image is in screen, and you've got lots of new extra space on the top and bottom.

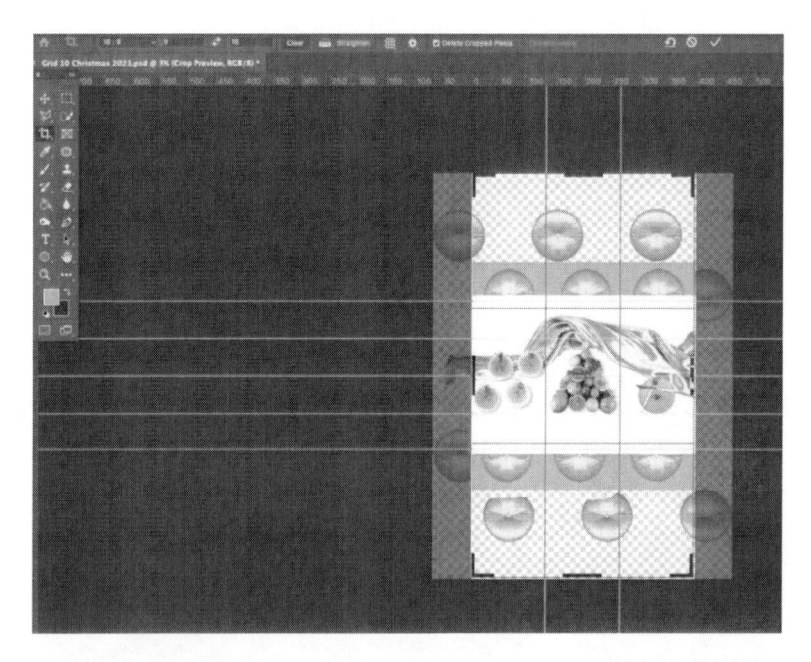

Fill in the top and bottom with a continuation of content or a flat colour (Note: some of this new area of image will be in view when someone goes to the Reels section of your profile)

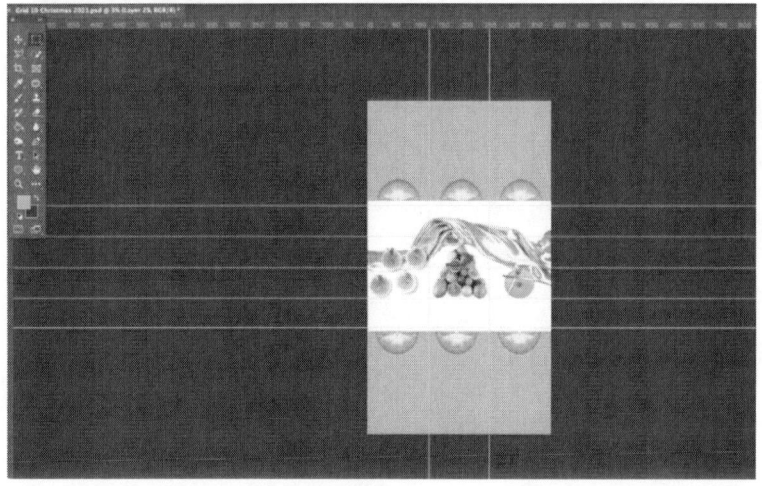

Last, you're going to hit crop again (should still be 9:16) and you're going to drag it to the width of your image. Center it on the center lines you added previously like below.

47

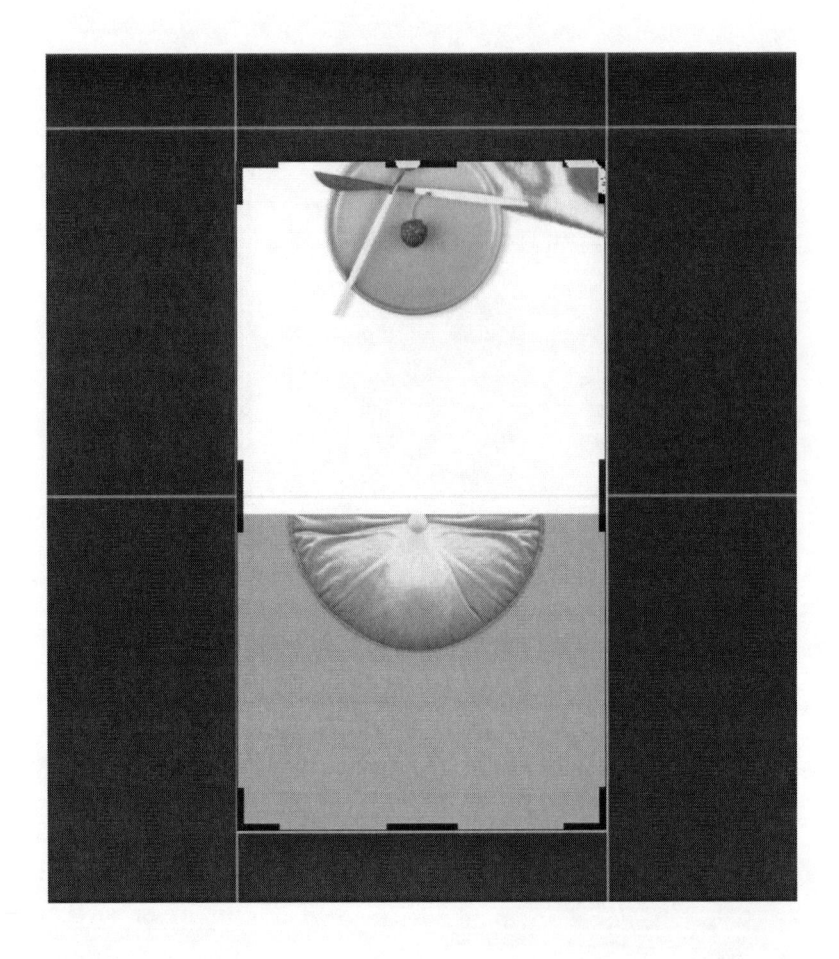

Save in order: 1-9.

Upload at the cover image for each of your Reels, you'll have super interesting content AND it will be a part of a 9 grid.

Social Media Strategy

So you've got your name, your team, your identity, and your tone established now, great. Next, you'll want to create profiles on all of the relevant platforms you're going to be on. Those platforms will differ from account to account – maybe you'll pick TikTok, Twitch and Instagram. It's up to you. For the average person starting out, I would recommend that you choose Instagram, Facebook, and TikTok. You can always reserve your usernames on all platforms, and decide if you want to build out those spaces later.

Once your basics are set up, you'll want to take a second look at your Instagram from the grid point of view. Your aesthetic grid strategy refers to the cohesiveness of your Instagram grid in totality, including your content, your bio, your highlight images, your business profile functions, and your profile image.

Set up:

1. Choose your platforms (TikTok, Instagram, Facebook, etc.)

2. Create imagery for all channels (profile image, cover photo)

    Pick a profile image that can be easily identifiable from a distance. This image is so tiny when you look at comments from your account. Your image shouldn't have too many details (if at all) and you should be able to see what it is even in the size when you comment on a photo. Try your band logo, a straight colour, or a pattern. I don't recommend a full band photo with more than one face in it. Try to be as consistent as you can with your profile image - don't change it too often. The same with your band name or handle.

3. Set up with correct categories & create highlights

    Add highlight images and make the covers fit your colour scheme (remember that colour scheme generator we talked about?). Make your highlight covers different colours that fit your aesthetic. Don't add text to them. Images are great, straight colours are great, don't make them just text. Once they have been uploaded and you have a highlight, you do **not** need to add a new image to your story in order to change your cover images. You simply need to edit that highlight.

4. Set your handles to be the same (Use namechekr.com to make sure your handles are available on all platforms quickly)

5. Submit for verification (Facebook)
    - Step 1: Go to your page then go to Settings. ...
    - Step 2: From "General" go to "Page Verification" and click "Edit."
    - Step 3: Verify the Page. Click "Verify this Page."
    - Step 4: Provide Business Phone Number or upload ID.

6. Switch to Business Profile on Instagram (this gives you better analytics).

    With a Business account on Instagram, you can add an "Email" option or a "Shop Now" option and link them with your website or your booking email. This is important - you want it to be as easy as possible for fans to buy your music/merch and for bookers to get in contact with you. Some of them prefer email because they can turn it off (the same reason why I don't like getting IG messages from some of y'all about class work). Respect the medium and be available in whatever way bookers want to find you. Do this part immediately as once you switch, you will loose your analytics. Best to do that while there isn't much going on.

7. Fill out your bios accurately and completely

Make sure your social bios are a condensed version of your full band bio. This means they should have key points that are directly from your full band bio. Don't just leave you bio blank - once you're actually famous, you can do that, but until then, you need to sell fans on why they should be following you. That's what your bio is about. Even if it's just emojis, have something, and make sure it relates back to your full band bio. Your Facebook bio can be longer, and as filled out as you can make it.

Your Instagram bio should be short and have the most important pieces of info. Ideally, it will be a 3-5 condensed form of your band bio. Your band bio is critical - when booking large shows, it's a mandatory marketing piece you have to provide with your EPK (electronic press kit). Your Instagram bio should have choice keywords taken from your band bio, so there's consistency. You need to let people know what kind of genre of music you are. If you're too cool for that (which idk you may be) it should be poetic or adding value to your music. Don't leave it blank (you're not a known artist yet, so you still need to work to introduce potential fans to your brand). Emoji's are a language, and you can use it in part or in whole for your Instagram bio if you choose.

Second, add a call to action. This means a signifier that asks your fans to do something. Ex. "Buy tickets below!", "Watch our new music video!" or "Buy Merch!" are all call to actions. You should only have one call to action in your bio.

"Buy Tickets to Our Release Show below! ⬇". Use your link for upcoming shows etc. It is not enough to say "music below" or tickets below". The psychology doesn't lie - you have to add an action in "**buy** tickets, **watch** our video, **listen** now". You only have one link, don't waste it. The only accounts that have access to more than 1 link on Instagram are either verified, or they have over 10K followers.

8. Create an email account just for the band

- With this new email account, update the private/back-up information for your Instagram, twitter, Tiktok, etc. If you get locked out, you should have easy access to that email account. Don't make the back-up info for your social accounts a personal band members info - this will be especially tricky if they ever leave on bad terms. Instead, give everyone access to the

53

band email, and change your password should you ever need to in the future.

Social Media Tools for Artists

In order to create a social media presence for your band or yourself as an artist, you need to start with the basics. Now many artists either skip these steps entirely or create their own version of some of these items, but it will save you **significant work and hardship** to download these specific apps instead. I've taken the time to sort them and clarify them for you. I'm sure that some will work differently on iPhone/iOS, but you get the general idea. There are 4 major different types of social media tools that you will require:

1. Project management
2. Social Media Scheduling
3. Maintenance
4. Analytics

Project Management

      a. Asana
      b. Google Calendar

These apps are the most important. This is where you stay organized with all members of your group or band, aka project management. This is most notably where you'll co-ordinate on your content calendar.

Your content calendar is literally a calendar of content that goes out on specific days, complete with an image, copy (caption) what platforms it's going out on (Instagram, Facebook, TikTok Twitter, Stories, etc.), and your content pillar or community pillar (this is the category of post that forms your content, of which we will go into further detail later on). A content calendar is highly useful if your social media manager is travelling or can't post that day, and someone else needs to. It allows the entire act or band to know exactly what needs to go out and on what days.

You can also use project management apps to schedule practices and other smaller tasks so everyone is on the same page. I like Asana because you can use it as both a content calendar, and as a project management tool. AKA you can have your regular content in there, but also add in tasks like "practice at 7PM bring the merch bin @ryan" and any members can get email notifications about it. There is an app version which is absolutely excellent - you can go into your project, click the date, and copy and paste the image and copy that is supposed to go out on Instagram easily. The one downside - if you create your content calendar in Asana, posts aren't actually scheduled to go out on Instagram, Facebook or TikTok. You still need to post them on those channels, or schedule them with another tool.

I recommend using Asana as your content calendar tool, and Google Calendar for shows/practices. Ultimately, it's up to you to try them out and see how you work best. You'll always get the odd person in your band that just won't check any of them. And that person is the worst.

Social Media Scheduling

      a. Native Scheduling
      b. Hootsuite
      c. Buffer

So as mentioned before, these are the tools that you can schedule your posts to go automatically post on specific times and dates. Scheduling in advance is a huge time saver, and you can get an entire month set up in less than an hour. The problem with these tools however, is that Instagram and Facebook have done a great job of rendering these tools a bit useless. Both Facebook and Instagram favor natively posting through their platforms, and Facebook has its own native scheduling platform entirely. If you are creating different content to go out on Instagram vs. Facebook, it makes more sense to schedule natively on Facebook and then post on Instagram natively anyway. If you're putting the same thing out across those integrated channels, you can share directly from Instagram to Facebook.

Hootsuite or Buffer can be useful if you want to mass schedule your content at the same time, and it's going out across multiple different platforms. I've experienced issues firsthand with Hootsuite where posts scheduled to go out on Instagram went out on the wrong accounts, which is an area of concern to be aware about if you manage multiple accounts through one Hootsuite account. Hootsuite is also very pricey after eliminating their free option (or perhaps it's hidden away somewhere, hard to tell). My opinion is that scheduling tools are on the way out, unless they take on other useful features such as becoming a content calendar or project management tool. My process is to upload everything to Asana, and have the team upload pieces of content to Tiktok, Instagram, Facebook etc from there.

Maintenance

    a.   Reports

Maintenance apps are apps that show you who unfollowed you, or doesn't follow you back. These apps suck and are plainly bad for your mental health. Just be prepared to get really upset. This app will show you which of the people you follow that don't follow you back. The first time you use this you will be genuinely surprised at the people who unfollow you. Don't take it to heart. I find especially with singer-songwriters who use their account for personal use and for music, a bunch of people you genuinely like in real-life may unfollow you. It's not personal. If anything, you advertise yourself as a person, but then it becomes more of a business (whether music is super formal or not). You need to do a cleanse before you start doing any kind of promotion, so you can keep these numbers as low as possible. You should use this app once a month to unfollow whatever followers unfollowed you (which you are still following).

Analytics & Reporting

      a.   Whatagraph

Whatagraph is a very expensive and useful tool for reporting. It lets you measure your social metrics and compare it to specific periods, and can be very useful for giving metrics to any key people that have invested in your group, or even to try to get grants or funding. They have a 30 day free period - get as much out of it as you can.

      b.   Fohr (Sign up as an influencer)

This website is an influencer management dashboard/tool. The reason I am suggesting you download it is because they've partnered with a very expensive analytics software that is probably the best out there, and you can have access to some of these analytics with a free influencer account. It also doesn't hurt if you'd like to open yourself up to sponsorships from brands down the road. Definitely sign up (but not as a brand, as an influencer).

      c.   Create your own

This is likely what you'll do once your Whatagraph trial has expired. Take the info that you found valuable from there, and create a Google Sheet. Add all of your info in a monthly format and update it every month. Track whatever is valuable to you - how many followers you grew on a monthly basis, best performing pieces of content, worst performing pieces of content, which content pillars did the best, which stories had the most views, etc.

Other apps we will cover later in this book for content creation:

Cinemagraph

Unfold

Skylab

Crave

Videoshop

VSCO

Face Tune

How to create a content strategy

Your content strategy is incredibly important. This is your plan for what content you're going to put out, how, and when. It shapes your content calendar, and also relates to how your social media presence looks. Here's a simple process to develop a content strategy.

1. Define your community pillars, or content pillars (See next chapter on this)

    Again, these are the categories or types of posts that go out. They should appeal to different groups that all have an interest in your brand. Ex you've got your loyal fans, your new fans, your friends and family. They may also be separated by age or geographic location. In some instances, it may be separated by a handful of content that went viral. You want to continue putting out social media content that is relevant to all demographics that follow you. Some examples of some generic content pillars are: Behind the Scenes, Member Spotlight, Live Shows, Throwbacks, etc.

2. Determine your mix of content

    You shouldn't be putting out an equal amount of posts for each group. Which is your biggest group? Your most excited group? The group that buys tickets, shows up, and shares your music with the most amount of people? You want to still be relatable to the rest of your communities, but make sure that your mix is proportionate.

3. Execute your filter or aesthetic treatment

    If you're having trouble with this part, find other Instagram feeds that you really like and pinpoint things you like. Your aesthetic treatment can be bright and punchy, or it can be dark and moody. It can be anything you want as long as it's consistent. Once you have a general idea of what it's going to look like, you can play with more advanced features such as larger grids using reels. Read more about this in the Aesthetic Strategy chapter/

4. Determine contextual events

    Example: holidays, Canadian music week, NXNE, Coachella, upcoming shows, band member birthdays, etc.

5. Determine posting frequency

    This should be more frequent when you're gearing up for a tour or a big release, and should be at least twice a week when you're just coasting. Stories should be posted as often as possible (at least once a day).

6. Determine a start date

Don't just put up a post before you're ready - it'll look worse that you started and couldn't keep up. Set a start date that's actually realistic.

Community Pillars

Community Pillars, also known as Content Pillars, describe the category of posts that make up your content. It's not enough to only have music videos or only have your music without an element of entertainment - and there a million different ways to do this creatively. You must have a healthy mix of types of content that appeal to that various different communities or demographics that follow you or your band. Community pillars will be very different depending on the act, but there are always a handful that most acts have in common.

Some generic examples:

- Live Shows
- Holidays/Contextual events
- Covers
- Music Videos
- Behind the Scenes
- Member Spotlights
- Show Promotion Incentives (Contests)

Going a step further, here are some really unique and entertaining categories that other musicians have used (with great success!) in the past.

Niche targeting

This strategy involves using the incredibly specific algorithm that belongs to TikTok. Canadian artist John Muirhead does an incredible job at this, by listing specific keywords that might link him to new fans. He lists other artists, his location, and has a clear call to action to "follow" if you're already a fan of those artists.

Songwriting Comedy

This strategy has been used by many, but really perfected by Tom Cardy and Natalie Burdick. Both of these artists create music **specifically** for this short form video purpose – not formatting it for TikTok but **creating** it for TikTok. The subject of this content is always about something dumb, mundane or hilarious, but set to really good production value and songwriting. The video is often low-fi, in Tom's case, always in what appears to be in his basement with whatever he happens to have on. It's super casual, which makes it feel way more relatable too. Natalie often will use the Greenscreen effect to make her content look like it was edited together in a few minutes, which again, feels super relatable. Neither of them takes their music too seriously, but it's a springboard for their careers. They are both quite well known now, and Tom has been touring. Either of them could pull a Doja Cat Bitch-I'm-a-Cow-to-Pop-Stardom at this point and would be widely successful.

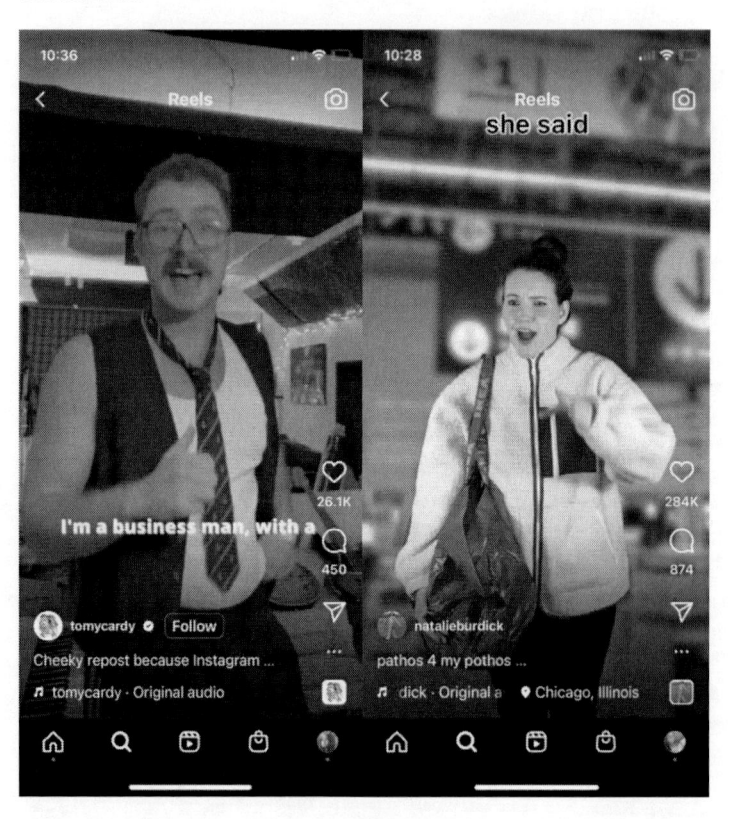

Whatever it is Lubalin was doing

IDK what to call this but it definitely gets its own genre. In art, there is a style called Readymade – where objects can be found and simply elevated to the status of art by calling it art. What

66

Lubalin does reminds me of this – he took content that was already funny – arguments on the internet – and set it to music. He wrote incredible melodies and produced it like it belonged in motion picture, all the while dramatically lip syncing along to his creation. Within days he was internet famous, and literally doing a collaboration with Jimmy Fallon and Alison Brie on The Tonight Show. Instead of continuing to create this type of content, he made a bit of an error – he let his popularity cool down while he rushed to put out original music that was different from what made him famous. His original strategy was brilliant, and if he doesn't pick that torch back up, I'm sure someone else will.

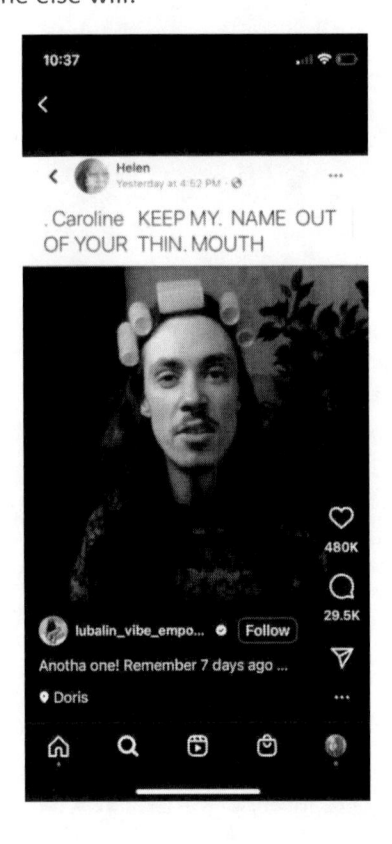

Using trending audio + contextual events

If you're going to use trending audio, make sure the context is absolutely on point. Many artists do this well, Haviah Mighty (Music Industry Arts Alum, Canadian!) does an incredible job of this, being timely, socially conscious, and super relatable.

-

Trivia

AKA ethical engagement baiting. Many artists do this well, but The Arkells and Brigit O'Regan do it best. Any kind of content creation that requires users to interact with a video for incentive will ultimately drive up organic reach for those videos.

68

An easy and tactful way to keep engagement high. I really like Brigit's method, as she hits a very specific niche of video game content/music. She will play a few notes and let people has it out in the comments as to what it is.

Songwriting Reactions

I've seen this done a million times, and I love it every single time. There are a few variations on this, and they usually take place in a car. The structure is always the same: "My girlfriend/friend/brother doesn't know about this song I wrote", watch to see their reaction because it's clearly about something that the other person has intimate knowledge of. Sometimes this is about exes, failed friendships, fuck-ups, etc., and the reaction of the other person in the car is what always drives up engagement on these, because its often super genuine, shocked, upset, or excited. I really loved Brooke Alexx's take on this, because her hook (below) immediately made me want to know what the song was about.

-

Trend Creation

This is by far the most difficult and impressive new community pillar you could attempt. That is creating music specifically to create an accompanying trend for TikTok and Reels. Qveen Herby is among the greats for this, as she is the genius behind several different huge Reels/Tiktok trends. Below is one that hasn't totally taken off (yet) and the concept and songwriting is

70

absolutely excellent. The track & production is an **absolute bop**, while her execution of video editing is perfectly Gen Z, and the concept (things ur dad didn't let u do cuz ur a girl) perfectly illustrates her lyrics. It's not over edited, it feels genuinely and like she literally made it – and it's already been used for audio in 1,432 reels. This, is impressive & incredibly well marketed.

-

These are simply some interesting and creative ideas that other artists have done. There is so much left to create. As new features are announced, the opportunities will change.

71

These categories (community pillars) should be spread evenly in your content calendar, unless you're having an absolute viral moment then you need to continue with whatever is working.

As touched on earlier on, your content calendar requires community pillars to label your posts, so you can see on a glance how many types of posts you have in a month. This allows you to make sure content is spread out evenly, but also allows you to look at bigger picture events such as holidays, or proximity to other events such as big shows or other important dates.

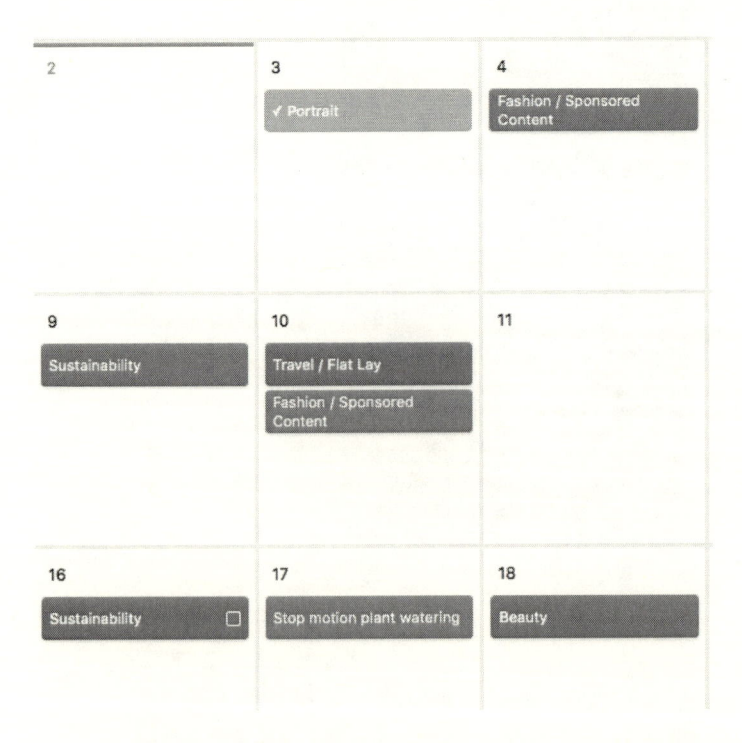

2	3	4
	✓ Portrait	Fashion / Sponsored Content
9	10	11
Sustainability	Travel / Flat Lay	
	Fashion / Sponsored Content	
16	17	18
Sustainability ☐	Stop motion plant watering	Beauty

As you create your calendar, you may find that certain posts don't fit perfectly inside one category or another. That's cool

72

too. You can have posts that are somewhere in between - as long as you're giving variety, so your fans don't get bored with the content you put out.

Not sure how to create your community pillars? Start by finding out more information about the people that follow you. You can always check your Business account insights, which will tell you information about your fans such as gender, age, and cities. There are many apps that you can use to find out more info, my favourite is definitely FOHR.

https://www.fohr.co

Sign up as an influencer, and you're doing two things. #1, you'll open yourself up to brand collaborations coming to you (instead of pursuing them yourself), and second, you have access to some really detailed analytics at no cost. Here are some of the details from my personal account in 2019:

Audience Gender

Male	Female
54.2%	45.8%

Audience Marital Status

Single	Married
55.1%	44.9%

Audience Parental Status

No Kids	Parent
83.5%	16.5%

Audience Religion

Christian	Jewish	Muslim
80.5%	10.3%	9.2%

Top Audience Countries

Canada	United States	United Kingdom	Nigeria	India	Brazil
43.9%	37.0%	4.0%	3.1%	1.2%	0.9%

Top Audience States

California	New York State	Florida	Texas	Georgia	Pennsylvania
14.9%	12.8%	10.4%	9.0%	5.9%	4.3%

Based on this information, I know that the majority of my followers are Caucasian, 18-34, with most falling between 21-24, with no kids, living in Canada. Half of them are married, and half of them are not. Also a fairly even split between male and female.

This app used to give much more detailed information about profession and income as well, but unfortunately it stopped offering that option earlier this year. I do know however that nearly 20% of my fans are musicians, 40% are in marketing, and the rest is spread out between other professions. This means that when creating my content calendar for the month, at least 20% of my content should be catered towards musicians. And that 40% of my content should be marketing related, or at least marketed well in a polished way. It also means that I should stay away from content that is focused around kids/family, so I can be a bit edgier with my content. It also means that posting about my own relationship could be very polarizing to my audience, as they are fairly split between who is in a relationship and who is not.

Optimizing Instagram Stories

Whenever you're posting stories, there are a few things to keep in mind. Otherwise anything else goes - it disappears after 24 hours so no need to overdo it. You want to have a minimum of one story per 24 hours. The ideal number of stories is 4-5 a day once people are very engaged.

Whenever you're shooting content, make sure that it's always optimized for portrait mode, so you can repurpose for stories. There is no real reason that you should be shooting content landscape anymore.

Try to incorporate motion wherever you can by shooting video, adding Instagram stickers, or turning your still images into cinemagraphs. Adding motion makes it significantly more interesting, even if nothing is really happening.

The purpose of stories is to create off the cuff, interesting content that is easy to digest. It also really helps your organic engagement. Engage your audience by using the poll functions, questions, this or that, etc. But don't offer two answers that are the same - always give your fans the chance to say they don't like something. You can also use this for really mundane things like "tea vs coffee" and it still really improves your organic reach of your posts.

This content should be daily, pop culture relevant, and does not need to be 100% branded. Should be fast, digestible and interesting. Don't have so many stories that you can't count (If the top of your screen looks like a bunch of little dots, you over did it.

Use the location function in every single story. We call this the tag and pull. It helps getting your stories seen, and if you don't like the way it looks you can simply drag it out of the frame and it will still register for that location.

Create highlights, with branded highlight cover images. This can be as simple as a solid colour – it's the easiest way to incorporate a colour scheme into your Instagram. It'll allow you to sort your highlights into essentially your community pillars. This might mean New Music Friday, Songwriting, Live Shows, Tour Dates, Muse, etc.

Using the example of New Music Friday, you might have someone from your team puts up a playlist and rotate through your team/band mates. It's a simple way to incorporate fluff content into your music, so fans can relate to you and your likes/dislikes. It's one of the most important parts of creating a die-hard fanbase.

How to Increase Ticket Attendance for Events Through Social Media - Organic

There are two different ways to increase ticket attendance for an event though social. One is organically, the other is paid.

Organic

1. Create a Facebook event - make sure all fields are filled out to the best of your ability. Create a custom graphic or video for the cover image. Make sure that video is short, and has a clear call to action to buy tickets to the show. Make sure you've made members of other acts who are also performing a host. If there's a promoter, make sure they're a host too.

2. Remember the Rule of Seven - consumers typically have to see an advertisement 7 times before they actually buy something. This applies to buying show tickets too. You want to make sure you're promoting your show at least 7 times, across different platforms. This may mean a post on FB, a couple of posts of IG, 4 stories, and maybe a contest for some free tickets through the venue's Instagram.

3. Be interesting. No posting show posters with no relevant information. I wish I could make this section bigger. Actually, you know what, I can.
   Don't just put up a show poster and expect people to show up.

That's not enough work. Why should they show up? Will it be more exciting than your lackluster marketing?

Some creative examples we saw this year was to make a Worlde, or a crossword puzzle
4. Make an eye spy
5. What are some community pillars we can use here?
6. Covers
7. Contests - hide tickets at local coffee shops, stores, pubs, etc.
8.

9. Give your event a branded name. This means picking a theme and sticking to it. Be as creative as possible. Come up with a colour scheme / font and a funny or interesting idea to run with it. Think about how Friends episode titles all start with "The one with". What would be your episode title? Make the theme or idea memorable enough that multiple different people would be able to name your show as "the one with" without ever having spoken to one another. The one with the pinatas everywhere. The one with framed photos of Dennis Rodman everywhere. The one that with a bunch of glow in the dark stuff. It doesn't matter what it is, just pick something.

10. Next, you'll want to use a breadth of different types of content to promote the show. Always include the show date (in every post) and the location, and the Facebook event URL (Facebook only, refer Insta fans to "link in bio). You'll want to post regularly with an event coming

up - every 2-3 days will be your sweet spot, depending on how big your audience is, and how large the show is. There are a million ways to do this, here's a suggestion of the most popular types you may want to post.

    d.   Show announcement post

>Include a cool visual or graphic with minimal text (so you can boost it later if you choose, we'll go over the Facebook 20% rule a bit later).

    e.   Show promotion (Incentive post)

>Introduce a specific reason why fans should show up (ex. incentive them with new material, candy, a cool display wall, free beer, seeing your band in a specific outfit, make a joke about a famous person going to show up etc.

    f.   Show promotion (Behind the scenes)

>Videos of the band talking about the event, setting up, creating a Snap filter, funny or interesting band rituals, etc. (Important, this DOES NOT include pictures of videos of you or anyone else changing your strings unless your bass belonged to Rick fricken Danko because that is boring and nobody cares about that shit)

g. Show promotion (Other acts)

> Content cross shared from other acts that are sharing the stage with you. It's good courtesy, but it can also give you access to their hard-earned fanbase as well.

h. Show promotion (Contest)

> Consider doing a giveaway for free tickets. Parameters could be to share the post, or tag a friend who they would bring. Remember that the value of whatever you're giving away has to be equal to what you're asking. AKA no one will share a post to their timelines in exchange for $10 tickets for a band they've never heard of before. Consider this step once you've done a bit of promotion first, otherwise the contest can flop, which is considerably worse than not launching it at all.

i. Show promotion (music)

> Posting a music video, a lyric video, a live off the floor, or even a shitty photo booth recording of a snippet of a song or cover can have massive impact for show promotion. Some folks may come out just because they saw a video that your front

man did and wanted to see more. Sometimes it's because they finally clicked on your music video because they wanted to know what the big deal was.

j. Show promotion (creative)

It can be literally anything as long as it links back to your main call to action.

k. Show promotion (media)

Cross posting media articles from well known publications, radio stations or magazines can land you serious referral points and kudos from on-the-fence fans

How to Increase Ticket Attendance for Events Through Social Media – Paid

There are two different ways to increase ticket attendance for an event though social. One is organically, the other is paid.

Paid

First, there's an incredible amount of free resources directly from Facebook. Here's a simple module, but there are tons of other Blueprint resources I highly recommend you check out.

https://www.facebook.com/business/learn/lessons/boost-your-event

1. Create a Facebook event

2. Include a website URL when creating your public event (and don't make it private, you won't be able to make it public later. You'll have to restart)

3. Boost Event
    - This turns it into an ad that can appear in people's News Feed.
    - Adds a Sponsored label at the top of the ad.

- Lets you include either a "Get tickets" or "Interested" button.

4. Determine which objective you're going to use. If you're trying to increase ticket sales and have already done significant organic marketing, use "Get Tickets" If you're trying to drive awareness for their event, you'll want to use the "Interested" button. This tests the waters for social sentiment and ad recall lift (number of people who will remember seeing your ad if asked). It's also important if you haven't already done enough promotion as it's easier to obtain "interested" clicks than to get ticket sales.

To boost an event, you need:

1. A Facebook Business Page (in order to manage your Page, it must be connected to your personal account). Don't create a fake profile to manage your page. You will have to use ID to confirm your identity and if you've used a fake name you won't be able to get back in.

2. A published event on your Page that's eligible to be boosted. Look for the blue Boost Event button. If this is a private event you won't be able to do it.

3. Access. If you create a Page, you'll be the admin by default and can run ads. If you didn't create the page, you need to be added as an admin, editor, moderator or advertiser.

4. Good creative. Facebook has a 20% text rule, which means if their software detects 20% or more text in your image, the ad won't run. So sayonara to your lonely show poster. You'll have to use something more interesting. I recommend a video, as you can always retarget those who watched a video for at least 15 seconds.

5. Target your audience. If you've run other events that are similar, you're in luck. You can simply retarget the people who went to previous events. It's a game changer. Don't bother with Interest targeting, it's the least effective way to advertise on Facebook. Pixel data is best. I won't go into this in this book, but again I recommend checking out Facebook Blueprint courses on this.

6. Budget and Duration. I suggested a minimum of $20/day. The learning phase for some ads can take a few days, so try to run it for at least a week if you can. Check in on it **daily** to ensure it's running and your parameters are correct. You'll want to run this simultaneously with organic content. Remember our rule of 7.

7. Have your community manager bookmark the ad if it's a **dark ad.** Meaning it's an ad that is not posted on your wall or Instagram grid. You'll need to keep an eye on it to respond to any comments on the ad itself.

Exploring Content Variations

Content variations are the various different types of content you can create and put out, and the variations of each type. This used to be more important when Instagram or Facebook valued different types of content, but now video is king. Marketers are putting a heavy push on video and motion related content, as Facebook and Instagram continue pushing videos for ad spaces. Tik Tok has created a clear case for video being the way of the future, and all other social platforms scrambled to follow suit. Some content variations include videos, GIFs, Cinemagraphs, Photos & Animation. There are tons more (memes, illusions, scenic, etc.)

Videos

This should be your default type of content. There are several ways to capture content for video. You can chop up a music video, you can hire a video production company, you can invest in a DSLR, you can buy an old school video camera, or you can create video from your phone. All of it works well right now. If having an analog part of your look and feel is important, then actual film might be the way to go. If you're going for a polished pop star kind of vibe, then styled video production might be pertinent. If you're not sure or don't know where to start, a smart phone will absolutely do the trick. You can turn on live photos if you don't have a lot of time, or simply take videos of small clips wherever possible in 9:16 and stitch videos together later. A more advanced strategy would involve creating your community pillars ahead of time and filming specific video clips for your regular content.

- In app Editing – there are a number of really amazing in-app filters and functions that you can use that can save you loads and loads of time. Snapchat is pretty widely known for having really excellent quality AR filters, which you could use to film an entire music video if you wanted to. The "Disney filter" (aka the Cartoon filter on Snapchat) is pretty cool if you want to have a relatable human face in your video content but aren't super comfortable with using your face for your own marketing. The neon filter on TikTok is another really cool one that essentially creates a neon shadow using sharp lines.

There are tons of apps out there that you could play with that can save you both time and money. TikTok actually has a function that will line up your previous shot with your camera, so if you're doing a time jump with a snap or a transition, you can do so while seeing exactly how the camera should be positioned. Reels is really the only one that doesn't have anything to offer in this department – and it would actually be safer to film your content on your phone and then upload it to reels, then film it natively within Reels as the surprise shutdown rate is unfortunately really high.

- Prisms – essentially holding an object on the outside of your camera to create a cool effect. Lomography is the art of taking photos with cheap analog cameras, which is a really really cool route to take. Toy lenses are particularly cool as they are plastic, not glass, which can give you some really interesting effects. Try shooting video with a toy lens on your camera. You can also try this by buying a CMYK cube, crystals, paper sheets, gels etc. One of my favourite hacks is the glass magnifying piece from the inside of a car headlight. It creates some really interesting stuff.

- External editing – for when you want to have more control over your content variations, try using another app or video editing software. You can try out any of the ones below or give Premiere Pro a try if you really want a specific look or feel.
    - Videoshop
    - CutStory for Instagram This is a layout editor
    - Unfold (also does video)
    - Intro Maker Effects Video Edit
    - Cinemagraph Pro

Animation

You can use so many different methods to create animation. There are tons of really advanced apps, or really simple ones you can start with. You can make looping GIFs through GIPHY or Photoshop. You can even make a really simply animation by literally making a flipbook. Good animation has become more popular in recent years, with many artists opting to hire designers for entire music videos start to finish. Some of the easier ones include:

- Photoshop
- Premier Pro
- Stop Motion Photography
- Flipbook

Some of the more advanced softwares include:

- Crello
- Adobe Animate
- Blender
- Toon Boom Harmony
- Etc.

Photos

- Portraits (images where a person is the main subject)

- Still Life (images where objects are the main subject)

- Flay Lay (images where objects are the main subject, taken from above)

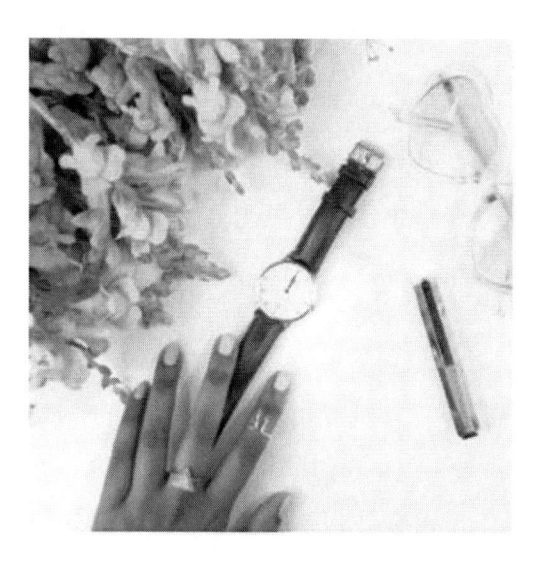

- Fantasy (images where content has been photoshopped to look fantastical or larger than life)

- Multiple Exposures (images that appear to have been taken on a SLR with more than one exposure in them, or edited to look this way)

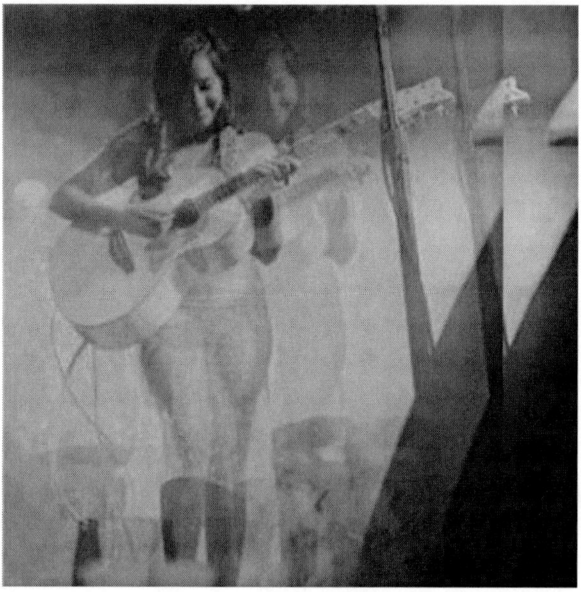

Interaction Online / Offline (Networking through Social)

Networking is the key to growing a social base for your act, and is instrumental in getting solid work in the music industry. This translates really across to all other industries, people value being referred by someone they already know and trust. If you can figure out a way to be trusted and known by multiple people in a specific friend group or specific music scene, you're bound to have success.

Networking online and offline can be very different experiences, but also can yield incredible results. The music industry is a small place. Knowing a lot of key players can really give you an advantage here.

When you're networking in real life, always wear something memorable so people can easily identify you and find you in a crowd. The guy with the yellow sweater. The girl with the hat. Etc.

This goes without saying, but be kind to everyone, not just people you think are industry professionals. If you are too cool to network, send someone on your behalf like a media rep or manager. If you're going to a show or a conference, aim to meet at least 5 people a day. Get their numbers, ask more questions than they do and let them do the talking. You want to know enough about someone that you could buy them a Christmas gift if you wanted to (but don't actually, just an exercise to know when you've sufficiently made a connection lol). And very, very important - don't ask for anything the first time you meet someone. It's super cringey and is disingenuous. Be genuinely interested in what they have to say, like you would making friends in real life.

If you run into a scenario where someone is rude or difficult to work with, see it through, and just avoid them in future. Don't write a blog about it or post about it. You will get destroyed online. I've seen difficult-to-work-with-people who remain in positions of power long after they've been called out for being difficult to work with. Sometimes being good at your job means that it's worth it for others to overlook rudeness. You don't need to tolerate it, but it's not worth it to throw your career over.

If someone is abusive or aggressive in a way that's not just them being a jerk - being ageist, sexist, racist, or otherwise discriminatory - it's a different scenario. Walk away and think about it before you and your fellow bandmates (if applicable) do or say anything about it and ask for advice from someone who is in a similar place of power. Think before you react. You would be surprised to find out you have more options than you think you do when you involve people you trust. Don't accuse, but you can ask for advice on what to do in that scenario. There will always be good people to help you if you ask.

Next, and this is a big one, don't expect other musicians to show up to your shows if you don't show up to theirs. Most of networking as a musician is just showing up to other shows. Be present in the music industry, especially in genres that are outside of your own. It's important to be known and seen as a community members, but you'll also gain so much insight and knowledge from watching different genres of musicians play.

Just get out there and experience it. If you're out at a bunch of different shows, you will be surprised who will come out to support you as well. It's a two way street until you've established a concrete fanbase. Who knows, you may also discover some really solid acts that you really like.

In the same vein, if you show up just for one act or ask about when a specific band is playing, other people notice. It's awkward as hell. Don't be that guy. If you have another commitment, it's okay, but don't make a habit of just showing up for your friend's set and that's it. You're not really going to glean much more out of that.

Growing a social following is a lot like gaining in popularity in real life - genuine interest, and reciprocation of effort works wonders.

Influencer Marketing & Product Placement

When it comes to influencer marketing for musicians, it's kind of weird that more artists don't do it. There's tons of money and brand affiliation that can be achieved through a solid brand partnership. Most brands have a PR company to do this for them - if you can't do that, here's where you start.

When do you want to start thinking about brand partnerships? As soon as possible. When do you want to start actually executing brand partnerships? Only when you're established, with a base of followers to work with.

Now there's an important distinction we have to make clearly here - influencer or affiliate marketing is not the same as requests to become a "brand ambassador" or to earn income off of a company's sales. This is not it. If you haven't heard of a company before and they are requesting a collaboration, google the company and google their product images with a quick image reverse search. You will find there are tons of companies making money off of people with this scam, where they resell items from Aliexpress or Alibaba at a 3000% markup, and use people who want to get into influencer marketing to do it. Don't fall victim to this. Not only will it hurt your brand, but it might ruin your chances of securing other brand partnerships. You want to secure solid brand partnerships that have quality products, services, and hold the same values and target demographic that you do.

Think about your brand, brand voice, and what brands would align with your marketing efforts.

Example: Grimes would be a weird match for a shop local Ontario Christmas campaign.

What brands are you interested in working with? Write them all down, and sort them in priority of best match to more abstract. Now create a second list, sorted in priority of most desirable, to least. If you're finding the partnerships you want the most are not even a close match to your musical persona, it might be time to do some rearranging of your current strategy.

Eliminate all the brands that are not a good match right now, and that are at the bottom of your priority list. These brands we can always come back to with a bit of prep and regrouping - but we're going to focus on the lowest hanging fruit first.

Before we move forward, any guesses what kind of partnerships will absolutely not be an option for you right away?

Gibson, Fender, Guild, Epiphone. You're not going to convince guitar brands to give you a sponsorship unless you are an absolute prodigy in your field. The exception to this is drum brands, if you're a drummer (and a really good drummer) I've seen a few drummers secure collabs and sponsorships.

Select 1-3 brands that you will be moving forward with. Know that this may not amount to absolutely anything, but this process typically works one out of 4 times you pitch it.

Think about the 3 brands you've picked and physically write out the branding terms that you feel that you share in common - for example if you're sharing a target demographic (teenage girls) in a regional area (GTA) and are both aiming to be body positive, inclusive, and cool.

Next, look at the calendar. What upcoming events, releases, or promotions could you possibly use a brand collaboration for? Some of the obvious ones:

- Music Videos / TV Spots
- shoes, jewelry, makeup, shirts, pants, hats, sunglasses, gear, perfume
- Album Release Shows
- Services like food, alcohol, pop-ups, also your promoter, even the venue itself for ticket or merch giveaways, other bands on the bill (do a giveaway of either merch, music, or an experience)
- Instagram or Facebook Live
- A local brewery that would sponsor free beer for you event with the mention of your name, fans can go pick up a case before the live
- Food delivery services or local restaurants
- Merch for on-air giveaways
- Equipment or service based sponsorships (Long & McQuade)
- Brands that you could offer product placement within the ad

Once you have a clear collaboration event in mind, start working on your pitch.

What do you bring to the table?

What access can you give them to their demographic?

While using numbers, what kind of impressions or reach can you generate based on a per $ amount by swapping services?

This is where we come back to that exercise we did at the very beginning of this book. Who is your target listener? What analytics can you pull to justify that you have fans that are also in their target demographic?

Next, you have to find an in, or a contact at this specific business that would be willing to talk to you. Specifically, a marketing manager, or someone who is in charge or PR, sponsorships or collaborations. Some companies get enough requests like this that they will have a separate department or email for it.

This is the tricky part. Being digital natives (most of you, I would think), finding information should be a lot easier for you. Think about that time you saw a cute girl or boy at a show and found her online in 46 seconds flat, or that time you went home from a party with someone else's right shoe and how you found them on Instagram within the hour. When you have a lead somewhere, you're guaranteed to find what you need if you look long enough. The internet has made that incredibly easy if you know exactly what (or who) you're looking for.

First step: Referral. This is the best option.

Try to rack your brain and figure out if you know someone who knows a person. You really don't want to use these resources often, otherwise people will be less inclined to support you overtime if you are constantly asking for something without providing something in return. As this is likely the first time you're doing this, it's ok. But be weary that sometimes overusing your connections can be dangerous territory. BUT If you look at Converse Canada's Instagram page and recognize a friend of a friend on their feed, that's a very good place to ask for a contact.

Second step: Google. This is a good option if you don't personally know anyone there.

Search for relevant Press Releases from that brand - you'll usually find a PR contact or email at the bottom. BINGO. Skip to the next step. If you haven't found them, time to go into a deeper dive.

Third step: LinkedIn. This is an OK option but chances are they won't respond to you here. This will help you figure out who you should be trying to get the attention of.

LinkedIn is the professional counterpart of Twitter. It's boring and dry and no one goes there unless they need something. In this case, someone. Search the company page directly, and see if they have their PR or Marketing person listed. You're bound to find something here.

Fourth step: Their Website. This is the absolute worst option. I'm only putting this here so you don't wonder why it's not on here.

You would think this would be the first place you would look, but the generic email addresses that brand's put up on their websites don't even come close to actually belonging to someone. You may be sitting in a pool of emails, unopened for weeks.

Now that we've got a contact, what the heck do we do?

We figure out a plan. First, get them to respond to you. Not to agree to a sponsorship, simply to respond to you. Think of like emails from brands that trick you into open them because you are acutely aware they are pretending to know you in real life. You can do this by

- Calling your contact by their first name
- Being extremely casual in your first touch - don't make it seem automated

- Point out something specific about the brand that you like

Hi Sarah, Kelly here. Love the new TTC ads with Millie Bobbie Brown x Converse! Walk past them every morning.

I'm trying to find the person who does brand sponsorships for an upcoming campaign with an artist I manage. Am I in the right place? Help!

Once your contact responds, go to the next step. If they don't - you have to get really creative to do so. Send them a funny GIF, or a blog article. My favourite is the minions GIF where he's getting hit in the face with a ping pong ball and not reacting. Older folks LOVE this shit.

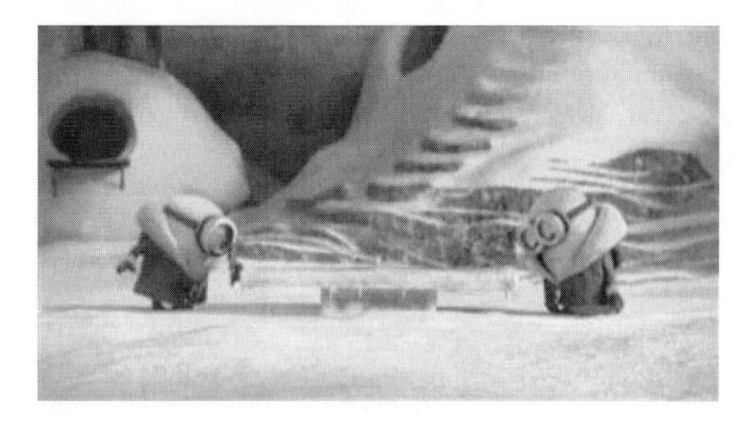

Uber eats some donuts to their office with a letter written on the top. Do what you can to stand out. If they still ignore you, time to repeat steps 1-4 again for a new contact.

I formed a relationship with Indie88 (a Toronto radio station) this way. We just asked if we could drop off some donuts. We taped our album to the inside of the box and it ended up meaning a contact there that eventually wrote a post about our album release. People LOVE eating things. It was the best $20 we ever spent.

Once you know who you're speaking to and they've responded to you, submit a collaboration request.

You want to tell them clearly what's in it for them, deadlines of when your project will be live or out, and when they can expect deliverables.

Hey Sarah, that's great, nice to meet you! The act is a singer/songwriter named Davis Mackinlay. Her target demographic is the same as the Millie Bobbie Brown campaign, and we can offer you key access to 14-21 females located in GTA, primarily Toronto ON. We're filming a new music video for her album single, "Roses", which is set to start production on Feb 24, and be released with a strong marketing push on June 4 2020. Our expected reach is 200,000, with an estimated ad recall of 4.0. We will be promoting this video through paid and organic Facebook ads, paid and organic Instagram ads, TV and Spotify ads.

Davis loves your brand and so we are only hoping for a gifted collaboration. Let me know if this interests you and your team.

Next, if this goes well, you thank them and send them your rates via a rate sheet.

Hi Sarah, sounds amazing! And just if you were interested, here's our rate sheet for other kinds of collaborations. Davis is so excited! Thank you.

Et, voila!

The important parts to follow:

- Keep your promises
- Keep your deadlines
- Reach out often and maintain those relationships
- Refer others to them as often as you can to show that you are a good contact to have as well.
- When actually placing product in videos, make sure there are several clear product shots that do not cut off the label or product, in any way shape or form. This also means ensuring that the product is lit well, and that the front (if applicable) is being shown.

You may want to ask the brand for any guidelines in working with their product, or any desired angles they would like it to be incorporated. Always ensure that it still fits your style, and that you're still aligned with your own branding.

Influencer Marketing Part ii

So you've secured an influencer marketing collaboration! Excellent. Here's what you need to do next.

1. Determine deadlines and deliverables

    If the brand doesn't give you a deadline, make one. This will make things a lot easier for you, and also make you look more professional for future campaigns. Commit to having all of your content by a certain date, and clarify what that content is. Do they want 1 feed post on Instagram and 1-3 Instagram stories? And then make sure you clarify - do they want approval before it goes live? And if they do, are you agreeing to unilaterally reshoot as many times as needed to get it right? With gifted exchanges, the norm is quite lax - they're not paying you for your time, so whatever content you choose to shoot and put up is at your discretion, which often means no approvals or reshoots. This often means they can't actually hold you liable to post a certain amount of pieces of content in exchange either - but you want to be courteous anyway. Say you'll create 2 stories and then put up 3. It's not a lot extra to secure a good brand relationship.

    When shooting your deliverables/content, make sure you're always keeping the product branding clear, unobstructed and in focus. This sometimes means you have to take more shots than usual. Consider the brands feed - the goal is to get reposted by them. If it's not good enough for their feed, it shouldn't be good enough for your feed either.

2. Determine key messaging from the brand

   This will usually come in the form of a campaign document or from your contact. It typically includes what new product or service they're trying to push, a call to action, a branded hashtag, and tagging #ad or #gifted. Although cringey, you must add the correct hashtag when posting sponsored content for legal reasons.

   The caveat to this - make sure it's still your own voice. You need to make sure you're promoting whatever they ask, but it should still be honest and authentically you. Don't go above and beyond promoting a brand if you are lukewarm about it.

3. Figure out where this post fits into your content calendar

   Make sure your deadline and your existing content calendar can exist well. This may mean rearranging some things so you don't have too many content-heavy posts back to back. You don't want your sponsored content to be posted too close to one another.

4. Determine content type

   Figure out what the heck type of content you're going to create. Are you going to try a stop-motion video? A cinemagraph? A straight up photo? Go back to the Types of Content Variations Chapter.

5. Write your copy

Make sure it's in your authentic voice, with their branded hashtags. Keep it short and sweet. Make sure someone edits it before it goes out.

Cool Instagram Features to Play With

Archive Function

This is a function that Instagram introduced so users could remove images from their profiles without deleting them. An example where you may use this - you've posted the wrong image, an image you've posted is getting a lot of heat because it was too controversial, or perhaps an older image isn't on brand with your aesthetic strategy anymore. Archived images can be added back to your profile whenever you choose, and will remain in the chronological order in which they were originally posted in.

A creative way to use the archive function: I created a countdown grid:

The "Game over" image was one of 10 countdown images, which counted down from 10, to 1, to the final image. I achieved this by posting all 19 images at the same time. First the #1, 2, 3, then #4, then I posted all 10 countdown images and after I posted each one, I immediately archived them. Very important - I did this at 3 in the morning so no one would see the ending. Then I posted the rest of the grid in order (#6, #7, #8 and #9). All I needed to do was to hit archive on the middle image, and then go to my archive folder, and select the image I wanted to display that day.

Content Style - Alternate D.O.F

Depth of field means the placement in the foreground, background, or mids. Regardless of whatever type of content you're putting out, you need to ensure the depth of field is

109

variated. Ex. Don't post two close-up portraits back to back unless it's intentional (ex. You're posting head shots of each band member)

Content Function - Carousel images

With carousel images, you can create a cool effect where it appears to be an elongated wide image where users can swipe between them to see the full image

The downside, you can't boost them (so don't do a carousel image for a tour release or anything that may require ad spend).

Content Tool - Filter Apps

An easy way to add an aesthetic to your grid without needing much work or planning is the use of a filter. Add a filter and go, or create a combination using a few features from a few apps.

- VSCO
- Face Tune
- Photoshop
- Lightroom

Content Tool - Manual Filters

- Introduce a colour
    - Borders (make them the same colour every time)
    - Uniform or clothing colour scheme (this one is really hard, because you essentially are styling your images. I would not recommend this unless you're really committed to a specific colour scheme.
    - Select painting / colour correct in photoshop or face tune
        - This option is great - the "paint" tool in face tune is a really rudimentary way to include a colour in an image. You are using your fingers however, so you don't have as much nuance as you may have in photoshop with a cursor.
        - Photoshop's colour replacement tool is supreme, but it's also a lot slower and not always necessary.
- View it in Grid format before you post to see how images look beside one another instead of posting it quickly and deleting it. You can use VSCO for this, or any other grid apps. Trust me, we all see it.

How to Increase Instagram Engagement

Instagram algorithms change constantly, which means this chapter constantly changes with those updates. To increase your engagement, 2 core things never seem to change. Engaging with others content, and posting consistently. The rules in which we do those two core items can be fairly complex.

Engaging with others content

l. Commenting on other photos
m. Liking other photos

Now, I am going to preface this section by clarifying that these findings are based on trial and error. I do not work for Instagram, nor do I know anyone who works for Instagram, so it's possible that you could attempt these and you won't have exactly the same result that I did.

So, let's start with who you're engaging with. You want to find users who are similar to the same users you want to follow and engage with you - your source accounts. As an artist, this is a bit easier. Create a list of bands that influence you, that you find your music similar to. Write them down somewhere. Now, you're going to check if their followers are purchased or not, because if followers are purchased, you can't be using them as a source account. You can do this several ways. First, go to their profile. Do they have 110K followers but only get 5 comments per post? If a profile has less than a 1% engagement rate, you know that it's probably bogus. So that account with 110K followers should be averaging at least 1100 likes for it to be legit.

Another way to check is to literally scroll through the followers and check the accounts - if the main language of the band or artist is English, but most of their supporters' bios are in Hindi, Russian or other languages, it's quite likely they have purchased bots or followers from like farms overseas.

Another way to check is through the use of third party apps such as Social Blade. If you can see a sharp surplus of followers in the last 30 days of 1,000, 5,000 or 10,000, chances are they are bought. There are other ways of explaining this of course - going viral, a contest etc., but if it's followed by a steep decline, you have reason to not use this account as a source.

Once you know your source accounts are legit, you can start commenting and liking on the photos of the fans of those source accounts. Extremely important - treat building fans on Instagram just like making friends in real life. You can't send the same mass text to 10 people you want to be friends with. It reads as super disingenuous. You have to leave real pieces of valuable feedback and comments. Don't use services that allow you to leave the same comment on 100 photos. Not only will you be caught by Instagram, it doesn't serve you at all. Instead aim to have 10 real conversations a day.

Some important things that you need to know based on recent algorithm changes:

- Video/Reels content is being prioritized over standalone images on both Instagram and Facebook
- Leaving emojis on posts is regarded as spam - if you're going to comment, make sure there's substance to it
- Liking the last 3 images of someone can be done by apps - don't use these services or your account may be banned
- Liking too many images too quickly can get your account banned
- Commenting the same thing on too many images can get your account banned
- Joining comment pods (groups on Instagram where you comment on each others photos) is against Instagram guidelines and seems to limit engagement
- Posting an image right before you engage with other people tends to increase your engagement on posts

Hashtag Research

Let's say the Community pillar you're creating a list is for Live Shows. You start at the basics - who and what.

Find record labels that you think would be interested in signing you. Find their branded hashtag by looking through their posts, or draft a comment anywhere and start typing out the name of the label, like this.

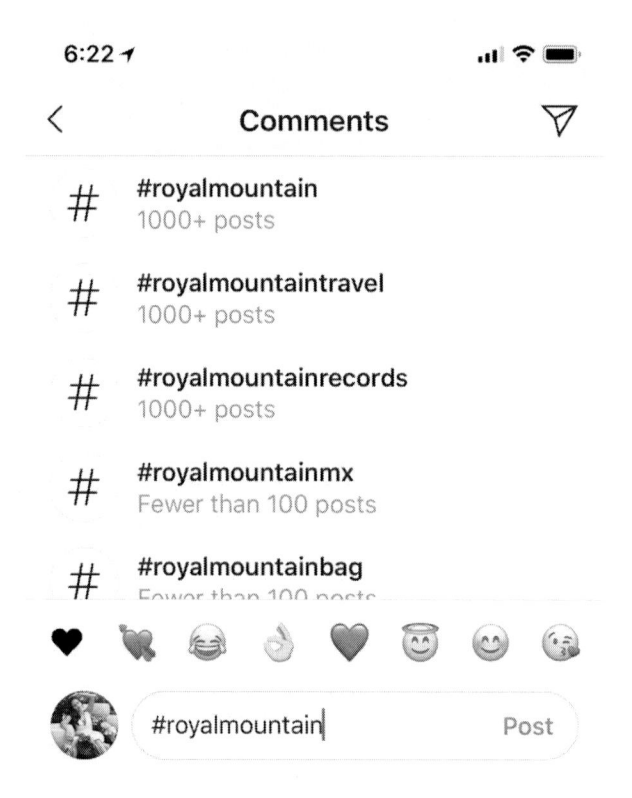

You'll want to be tagging at least a handful (2-3) of labels in every post.

Next, tag some genre choices and radio stations. These hashtags will likely be pretty huge, but also useful to being seen by new people.

Next, you want to find branded hashtags that pertain to your image or video. This means hashtags that companies or brands follow to use for reposting. Sometimes they'll be literally just the brand name, sometimes it'll be more complex. For example, if your image has a Gibson guitar, use the branded hashtag #Gibson, which you can find as its in their bio.

```
1:30                              ..ll LTE

<          gibsonguitar ✓              ...

 [Gibson]    1,475     2.4M      135
             Posts    Followers Following

Gibson
Product/Service
Legendary, Iconic. Dedicated to quality,
craftsmanship, innovation and sound
excellence since 1894. #gibson
www.gibson.com/gibsontv
```

Next, you'll want to add a bunch of micro hashtags - things that are specific and people may sort through. #ldnontario, #gtatour, your own branded hashtag, etc. These are the hashtags which

116

will rotate and change when you use this list again on another photo. Keep in mind - you can only use 30 hashtags per post. If you hit post and you've used more than 30, it will give you an error message, and you can't go back and edit that comment. Before you hit post, copy your hashtags and open up the notes app on your phone. Copy and paste them here. It's the most convenient way to access your hashtag lists and come back to them where necessary.

So how do you know if they are working? You'll want to check your insight on the regular to see where your hashtags place in terms of total accounts reached. If you're reaching at least 30% new people through your hashtag strategy, you're in good shape. Keeping in mind - some pillars will naturally have better traction on hashtags than others. It doesn't mean you stop using those hashtags - but you will need to revise them along as you go.

8:43	...

Post Insights

Interactions ⓘ

379
Actions taken from this post

Profile Visits	379
Website Clicks	4

Discovery ⓘ

9,838
Accounts reached
79% weren't following you

Follows	19
Reach	9,838
Impressions	10,708
From Hashtags	7,557
From Home	2,410
From Explore	30
From Other	711

This is where your post was seen the most. It got the most impressions from Hashtags, Home and Explore.

The big question - can we see which hashtags generated the most views or likes for my images? No, you cannot. If you find an app that appears to do this, let me know. Until then we're just going to use the good old fashioned trial and error method. Try using a list of hashtags for one community pillar and then adjust just 1 hashtag every time - you may find your best performing hashtags this way.

Last, which I just barely mentioned - your branded hashtag. You need to make one. This is how you can sort through content that your fans take, and also determine who to reward of your most loyal social followers. Get creative, make sure it's short, easy to spell, and that no one else is using it - extremely important. Once you've come up with it, add it to your bio. Encourage people to use it at shows. Add it to your business cards or stickers. Try to make it the same as your handle if you can. One word of advice - don't do what I did and make your handle or hashtag a word that sounds stupid to say out loud so you have to sound it out phonetically every goddamn time (@oatccband)

Checklist for Going Live

In the age of COVID, teaching you how to promote a live concert is a bit of a bad joke. Many musicians have successfully pivoted into live streams instead, whether on Facebook or Instagram. While I am by no means an expert on the subject, here is a short checklist of things to do before going live.

1. Have a rehearsal live. Test your audio quality in the exact room you're going to go live in, with the exact equipment and exact audio.
2. Go tethered if you can instead of a DSLR instead of your computer camera. There are many ways to do this using a secure key. I will provide a few links for this after this lecture.
3. Schedule your live so you can have an Announcement preview post
4. Put users to "Get Reminder" as the call to action.
5. Turn on auto-generated captions for those who aren't sure they want to commit just yet (& for non native English speakers)
6. Tie in a physical element if possible - Offer to mail out a set list or a secret invitation. If you want to be SUPER extra and got the extra mile, scent is a really strong element of nostalgia and memory. Spray your setlists with a specific perfume or include lavender etc. to create a very strong sensory experience that extends past digital.
7. Involve your audience - suggest that they all get a specific drink, or wear a specific colour, or do some specific ritual to be prepared - listen to a specific album or some other thing that will tie you all together.

"Welcome to Sleepless in Hawaii's streaming Luau. Get your favourite Hawaiian shirt on, and join us for an evening of tunes." Aim to foster an environment that extends past your music.

8. Sending out sheet music, lyrics, or a themed Sodoku

Video Strategy

Having a solid video strategy used to be a bonus to a solid marketing plan – now it's kind of the backbone of one. TikTok has changed the way we view social media, and both Instagram and Facebook have followed suit by developing their own versions of small format, smartphone first, video content. Reels & TikTok need to be a very important and very separate part of your organic social media strategy.

Some engaging ways to write a hook:

- Make the intro risky (sexual or dangerous)
- Tell them to stop scrolling (sometimes not effective)
- Ask them to wait till the end
- Include a confusing first screen grab that requires explanation (stroke simulations)
- Be overly excited (What I recommend) (addison rae)
- Create a Looping video

Some ways to be specifically engaging to the platform

- Use native filters
- Being emotional
- Use native sounds
- Use native trends
- Always shoot in 9:16
- Shoot in App
- Don't increase production quality
- Be short
- Be aware of attention spans

Music videos

Social media is no longer prioritizing full videos anymore. Instead of posting a link that teases a full music video on Youtube, try cutting up your music video into chunks that are all viewable without exiting the app. You can still upload the full video on Youtube if you wish, but make sure that fans can watch it without ever exiting Instagram, or TikTok.

There are 3 types of music related video promotion that really works on tiktok:

1. This is my girlfriend/boyfriend, and this is their dream etc. This is very much a behind the scenes where someone else is telling the audience: blow this up because I'm so proud of them. It elicits a strong emotional response and people are always hoping to help.
2. In the car (I got you played on the radio, reaction to songwriting etc (check the community pillars chapter for more on this)
3. In the car behind the scenes (this is a song I wrote it's about this this and this)

Thankfully, both platforms have made it incredibly easy to get started, and you don't need to be a marketing genius to do it. The rudimentary way to get good engagement and noticed is simply to hop on trends. Trends come in the form of dances, audio, filters, or storytelling. We've all seen a version of a trend that was clever and didn't require a lot of resources to do it – you can use the greenscreen filter to place you just about anywhere. You can lip sync over someone else's audio to tell a story you're not a part of. Or you can learn a dance or if you can do it.

The second level to this is creating a trend, by asking users to either stitch on TikTok, or to recreate on Instagram. Some formats for this are "Tell me about a time that _____" or "Tell me about your favourite _____". You can come up with just about anything.

Going past trends, is the gold content. The stuff that probably would have existed on vine if it were still around – stuff that is creative, weird, or otherwise incredibly entertaining. My favourite examples of musicians who have perfected their video strategies are @tomcardy & @natalieburdick. Their strategies are fairly similar – make a song out of something mundane or super specific. It's short, entertaining, low production value, and ALSO an absolute bop. We're talking songs that are specifically crafted for social media, that are less than a minute in length. They also all loop – the track feels like it doesn't have a discernable start or end. They're clearly having a great time, and are launching their music careers out of these little bits of B roll songwriting content.

If merging comedy with music isn't within your brand, apply the exact same rules to the kinds of imagery that are on brand for you. Going for the wanderlust thing? Put up a series of reels with your music playing over abstract scenes in cars, on the beach, walking in water, etc. You can be cinematic if you'd like – it just needs to be less than a minute long.

Viral Marketing Techniques

These techniques change constantly, but at the moment here are some tried and tested ways to go viral.

The easiest way to go viral used to be to make a meme. Memes are dead in their current form, and have been replaced by video content, or simple cultural terms that tie us together, like pandemi lovato or the panzeratti or how everyone is making fun of that guy on reddit for his insane "lovemaking" playlist. But the method for making a viral meme can still be applied to your regular content.

In order for it to go viral, it has to have the perfect mix of impeccable timing, risky content, and relatability to a niche market. For example, there was a girl who climbed a crane in Toronto a couple of years ago. She was all over the news for days. At the agency, we created a meme that related the top of the crane to housing prices in Toronto. It was the same day that news outlets couldn't stop talking about her. The risk laid in why she had climbed the crane - it wasn't very clear if she was just a daredevil or if she was mentally ill. It was a huge risk at the time and I did have a few people come for me on linked in - when it came out she was just a thrill seeker I was very relieved.

1 cozy apartment. Top Floor.
small but great view of the city.
no pets. no couples.
$1700 + Utilities

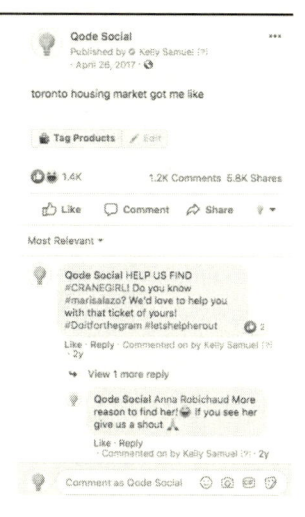

The relatable bit that unified our niche market (young people in Toronto) was the feeling of exasperation regarding the Toronto housing market. It was an outrageous example that matched some of the crazy expensive pricing and tiny, uninhabitable units that are climbing in price in Toronto.

This meme was seen by nearly a million times.

A better example would be this TikTok by Lubalin who blew up and ended up getting Jimmy Fallon on it, or this TikTok made by Trevor Dubois:

https://tinyurl.com/xt2t6uw6

This went well because it unified a specific audience that was niche enough to have common values, but large enough for it to go viral (Gen Z), it was pretty silly, timing was excellent because TikTok is very new, and there isn't too much social commentary yet about it vs. Instagram, and it was risky in how it slightly pitted Trevor (the underdog, Gen Z) against his boss (Millennial, me). This discourse is a really popular one and you should feel free to use it in a playful way.

This was seen 3.0Million times, and gained 100K followers in 5 months. We reposted it once.

Try to hop on regular trends in hopes that your content will be swept up in the current of what's popular. Some recent trends include the trend of making regular everyday content into music like Lubalin, Natalie Burdick, or Tom Cardy, or the countless TikTok trends that are thankfully no longer dance related. I'm going to take a moment right now and clarify that Tik Tok is by far the easiest platform to go viral on right now. If you have time, create as much content as you can. Chances are that something is going to take off. Try your hand at one of the trending videos like Flip the switch or that weird one that proves that men can't lift anything if their chin is being pushed up on. We haven't had any new platforms that broke through into mainstream use for North America since Vero attempted (and failed miserably) back in 2018, and debatably Clubhouse in 2021. This is a big deal. Instagram celebrated 10 years back in October. That means that if we're in the infancy stages of a new app right now, this is the time to get on it. By the time their algorithms are established and ads saturate everything, it'll be far more difficult to go viral.

Contests or Giveaways are an excellent way for something to go viral, but it has to be worth the social ask. If you're asking users to share something on their own feeds as an entry, the perceived value needs to be anywhere between $200-$500 for Facebook, and $500-$1500 for Instagram. Inviting others to tag a friend is a lower stakes entry option, or sharing to their stories. If you do a contest or giveaway, make sure it's actually worth the entry. You can do a bundle giveaway of $100 of a CD, shirt and an experience or free show tickets etc., or just tickets even, but the stakes should be relatively low and the barrier to entry fairly easy you get as many entries as possible. I always suggest to giveaway tickets a week before a big show, and ask users to answer a question like their favourite track or to tag a friend they would bring with them.

Shocking or emotionally stimulating content is another kind of content that can go viral very easily, and I'm going to say that as a bit of a disclaimer. If you're trying to approach people sentimentally be cautioned - if it's not for the right reasons or it's inauthentic, people will know. So don't make a post about a cause you don't really care about just to get the engagement - it will backfire, and it's kind of garbage to do so. But if there is something you care about it, the more intimate, the better. People really resonate with vulnerability, especially if you're opening up about how something happening in the world is affecting you. There's no better time to fight for the rights of others. So talk about the war against the Uyghurs, The Residential School System, Afghanistan, or the Wet'suwet'en. These are enormous global issues that will 100% introduce you to larger groups of people. It sometimes will also make you a target for internet trolls. Depends on how you want to approach it, but my philosophy is that if you have a platform, use it.

Funny/creative. The best example of this would be Walk Off the Earth playing that frickin guitar. When that went viral they went from a local Burlington band, to a wider known internet sensation. And they kept doing these damn videos because they work, even though they're super cringey now. Try something a little abnormal. If there's no risk involved, there's no chance it will go viral. So try something a little out of your comfort zone. Try a funny video. Try a new persona. Tom Cardy does a really good job of coming up with new and interesting musical content on the regular. Highly recommend checking him out.

Marketing Merch Online

There are a two major ways people can buy your merch:

Online

In Person

Online AKA E-commerce

This means that they're purchasing online with a credit card and the product will have to be shipped or picked up.

First you will need an e-commerce platform. This is a space where users can buy items with a secured payment gateway. The most common for artists and bands is Bandcamp. There is also Shopify or WooCommerce. I would recommend sticking with Bandcamp unless you're moving tons of merch. The difference is your annual fees as well as the percentage of sales. Bandcamp will take a percentage of your sales, but won't charge you any extra fees to have an account and a page set up. Whereas WooCommerce or Shopify may have less percentages, you're paying monthly or annual fees that can be quite large for a small band or artist.

Next, you're going to need to know how to price your items. This part is fairly simple - look around and see what the average cost is for similar items with artists within your caliber. If a T-shirt is going for $10, then that's fine on a small-scale level. But if you're selling tons of merch, you should determine what your breakeven is for your cost, aka how many shirts or CDS you need to sell until you get your initial payment back. If you spent $240 CAD on a short run of 30 shirts, your cost per item is $8. If you're selling your shirts at $10 each, you'll need to sell 24 in order to make your money back, and you only serve to profit $60 total. That's not a lot of money. In the normal business world, you should be doubling the mark up on your cost so it includes your advertising and actually making a bit of cash. The music industry doesn't work this way for whatever reason, but I want to encourage you to increase your goddamn prices. If you increase your shirt price to $15, the most you'll make is $450 which is a $210 profit, which allows you to invest back into your band for more EPs, stickers, or other merch items.

Alright so you have your merch, you have your e-commerce platform, you know what you want to sell them for, what next? Your visuals. You need at least 2 different images of your merch. One should be your very clean render or shot in white photo. When you make an order with most t-shirt companies, they'll give you a render of what the shirts will look like. Literally copy that image and upload it as your main photo for that product. See below.

This Jenny Lewis T is very likely just a render - the image photoshopped directly onto a plain white t-shirt. If your t-shirt company doesn't do this, you can easily do it yourself. The exact same goes for your album, vinyl, or EP. You want it to be clean, bright, and immediately identifiable. A quick and easy render.

Creative option

This will not be for everyone, but try tweaking the plain white render a bit by making these standard product images GIFs. You can add a touch of illustration or a blinking sticker or something. I'm not sure if Bandcamp even supports GIFS as a supported file type, but I've seen some stores do this and it's super cool*

All of the images after this should be actual images of the product being worn or contextually in a space. For a t-shirt, have a couple of friends model your merch. It can be in the same aesthetic as your Instagram feed even - which is what we call lifestyle. Make sure you have representation here - male and female models at the minimum, but even better to show your shirts on different body sizes, skin tones etc. If these images fit your IG, it's an added bonus, because you can then post them there and add a call to action to buy a shirt. We'll come back to this later.

Next, is the copy. Give as much information as you can in the description. Tell them what kind of fabric it is, what sizes it's available in, etc. But you want to manufacture demand so people buy them quickly. Think of this great toilet paper shortage of COVID 2020 - no one wants the option to buy to be taken away from them, so people panic when they know there's short supply. Try playing around with *LIMITED EDITION* in your title, or *SHORT RUN, WHILE SUPPLIES LAST*. These are tried and tested marketing techniques to get people to buy products quickly. This works best if you have an evergreen (always there) merch item that sells consistently and will always be available too, so people know that you may actually cut another t-shirt design from your roster.

Now that we have our product up and available for purchase, we need to find avenues to actually market it. The main ones are Facebook and Instagram, but as I mentioned at the beginning of this year, I think Tik Tok will be next.

Next, create a Facebook Shop and add your merch items to it. This can be done by using an API. Depending on your e-commerce platform, you may need to do this portion manually. I won't explain the technicalities of how to do this, but you can learn more through Facebook:
https://www.facebook.com/business/help/912190892201033?id=206236483305742

Once you've created a Facebook shop, you can actually tag products on both Facebook and Instagram posts. On Instagram from the grid perspective, that image will now have a small shopping bag icon beside it, so users are prompted to enter the purchase funnel. A user can tag the image, see the price, and go directly to the purchasing point.

From this juncture, just make sure to pepper in pieces of content that include your merch in a cool, creative, and on brand way. Don't just put up your render photos on Instagram, make it come alive with personality. Make it fit into your feed aesthetic.

The easier way to generate income for any business, musicians included, is to run ads. But after we did the math early, you can see that there's not a huge margin on merch. If 30 shirts cost you $240, and the most you can make is $210, it's not likely that you're going to spend $200 on ads. If you have 1,000 shirts, then absolutely this is a good option to consider. You can also run Google remarketing ads, which are those ads that once you click a product and navigate away from the page, you see ads for that exact product everywhere. Facebook also has a version in Audience Network. There is a saying, "you have to spend money to make money". It's 100% true.

Another avenue, always honour your loyal fans. Come up with some kind of creative thank you whenever you see someone wearing your merch online, or if they tag you. Such as a free B sides or stickers that can only be received if you post a photo online of you in the shirt, or a personalized song, or a shout out, free tickets for a show, etc. Give your fans an incentive to want to proudly wear your shirt and for you to see it.

The step further is giving your merch to important people that you think would actually wear it. Emphasis on them actually wearing it. If you can get in front of all the key promoters for the GTA and give them a CD and a t-shirt, chances are that you'll get significantly increased brand awareness which leads to more bookings, more streams, more money. This is Influencer Marketing in the reverse. Many brands will pay influencers to wear and promote their product. This is a route you can take as well, but instead of paying them it may have to be an in-kind trade - they wear your shirt in their next Instagram live that gets seen by 5,000 people, you get them guest listed for any show they want to come to that year. Get creative. Use a call to action. Be on all the relevant platforms.

Optimizing Your Tour Online

First step of optimizing your tour online - booking one. Do NOT start marketing a tour if you have not completed writing songs, recording your album or EP or booked your hometown venue. I cannot tell you how many people I know that jumped into their tour and thought they would figure out the logistics later and ended up looking really stupid. It also hurts your relationships with venues because they look unprofessional too. Trust me - your album or EP release can wait until you have the item physically in your hands - don't book a venue based on estimated shipping times or when your engineer thinks you'll be done by – just don't do it. A million things could go wrong between then and now.

Second step, give your tour a name. Something memorable. Treat it like its own little commercial or ad. It needs a name, a colour scheme, and some visuals to accompany it. If you're going out east, try a maritime-related pun or phrase. Or try something descriptive, or name it after the album you're releasing - whatever it is, make sure that you've named it and that it's memorable.

Third, make a poster and some accompanying merch for that tour, and make it a short run. Posters are a really great and low-cost thing to give away to promoters at the end of the night, as a thanks for hosting you, or folks you meet along the way that help or go above and beyond in supporting you. You'll want to post this puppy on Facebook and encourage people to share it or tag themselves in it however you can. Specifically on Facebook, as this is where the Events tab lives, and people tend to make actual calendar decisions here much more often than

Instagram. I'm sure this will change as your demographic ages but this is what works for now. Some ways I've used to get your poster to go viral - ask your fans to comment with their favourite track or tag a pal to be entered in a draw for free tickets to any show, a t-shirt and an album. The key here is that you need your post to go viral, so you can't be splitting your engagement and impressions with an identical post somewhere else. Instead of having your band members share it, you want to actually add their names into the caption of the original posts, so it shows up on their timelines instead of as a shared post. Engagement and growth are exponential, so the more people you can get liking your one post, opposed to a handful of people liking a handful of shared posts, the farther potential it has to be seen. It also gives you a good idea of what shows you can expect your friends to support you at.

Next, set up your Facebook events. You'll want to create a custom video header (if you have the resources to do so) for each show. This should have the venue, date, ticket price, time, + whatever other headlining acts on it. If you can, try to include a bit of performance footage or a snippet of a music video. You're aiming to sell them on the show in the first 3 seconds of them getting an invite to the event.

Next, ask your promoter if there is a budget to promote it. You can do so very politely by asking "Hey ____, the Facebook event is live now. Just added you as an admin. Would you like advertiser rights to promote the show? Or we can boost it if you'd like. Let us know. We've been told $50 is a good budget for a 2 day period. You can also do the math here by determining what the max capacity of the venue is, and the probability there is of selling it out. The last show I did ads for at

Lee's Palace, we knew capacity was 550, and organically we likely had about 150-200 people that were going to be there. We sold an additional 200 tickets at $10 each, which is an additional $2,000. That was with a $250 ad spend. If you're confident in your music and your draw, asking for a bit of ad spend usually paves the way for more money for everyone involved. I wouldn't recommend setting up the ads yourself though - pay someone who's done it before to do it for you, or try it out yourself with a much smaller risk venue and budget (like $50). To do an ad like this, you want to make sure it's quick. exciting, fun and above all that it's a video, for two reasons. #1. They're prioritized by Facebook for views and #2. You can retarget users who watched at least 3 seconds of your videos, which you cannot do if you use a photo. It also can capture the magic of a live performance a lot better than a still image can.

Next, you want to incorporate your tour content into your organic social media. Don't, and I repeat, do not just upload the tour poster on Instagram. No one can read it and it looks so freaking ugly on your feed. Please don't do it. Instead, consider incorporating it into an image somehow, and separating the tour dates into individual posts. Remember, someone has to see something 7 times before they remember it. If you're posting your poster on Facebook, twice in Insta Stories, that leaves 4 posts on IG before we've hit our baseline. When you're famous and successful you won't have to hustle quite this much, but unless you're freaking Haviah Mighty, we all have to play by the rules.

Promoting through Radio/Social

Alright! Here's a tip from my college radio days at 94.9FM. You need to get on the radar of specific shows at specific college radio stations, and also check your plays online. You can do so by checking https://www.earshot-online.com/.

Start with your city - if you don't know the college radio stations in your city, start there. From the earshot homepage, go to Stations, and see which artists are getting the most airplay. You may be surprised that you're already charting in specific locations. For some radio stations, it only takes being played **once or twice** to actually show up on these charts. This means that if you can talk to at least 3 radio station hosts per city, you can almost guarantee a spot on the charts.

From here, you'll want to check out individual radio stations - I recommend doing this in conjunction with a tour, and reaching out for a request for an interview at the same time. Once you know which radio stations you're going to reach out to, find shows that work within your genre, and find them on IG, twitter or FB. Wherever they're active. You want to make sure they know who you are. Like their content. Comment on their content. Create a conversation well before you ask them to do anything for you.

Here's the full list of college radio stations across Canada, courtesy of Wikipedia.

Call sign	Frequency	City of license	Owner
Alberta			
CJSW-FM	90.9 FM	Calgary	University of Calgary
CJSR-FM	88.5 FM	Edmonton	University of Alberta
CKXU-FM	88.3 FM	Lethbridge	University of Lethbridge
British Columbia			
CIVL-FM	101.7 FM	Abbotsford	University of the Fraser Valley
CFML-FM	107.9 FM	Burnaby	British Columbia Institute of Technology
CJSF-FM	90.1 FM	Burnaby	Simon Fraser University
CFBX-FM	92.5 FM	Kamloops	Thompson Rivers University
CHLY-FM	101.7 FM	Nanaimo	Vancouver Island University
CFUR-FM	88.7 FM	Prince George	University of Northern British Columbia
CITR-FM	101.9 FM	Vancouver	University of British Columbia

144

CFUV-FM	101.9 FM	Victoria	University of Victoria
Manitoba			
CJJJ-FM	106.5 FM	Brandon	Assiniboine Community College
CJUM-FM	101.5 FM	Winnipeg	University of Manitoba
CKUW-FM	95.9 FM	Winnipeg	University of Winnipeg
New Brunswick			
CHSR-FM	97.9 FM	Fredericton	University of New Brunswick
CKUM-FM	93.5 FM	Moncton	Université de Moncton
CHMA-FM	106.9 FM	Sackville	Mount Allison University
CFMH-FM	107.3 FM	Saint John	University of New Brunswick - Saint John
Newfoundland and Labrador			
CHMR-FM	93.5 FM	St. John's	Memorial University of Newfoundland

145

Nova Scotia			
CFXU-FM	93.3 FM	Antigonish	St. Francis Xavier University
CKDU-FM	88.1 FM	Halifax	Dalhousie University
CJBU-FM	107.3 FM	Cape Breton Regional Municipality	Cape Breton University
Ontario			
CJLX-FM	91.3 FM	Belleville	Loyalist College
CFRU-FM	93.3 FM	Guelph	University of Guelph
CFMU-FM	93.3 FM	Hamilton	McMaster University
CIOI-FM	101.5 FM	Hamilton	Mohawk College
CJIQ-FM	88.3 FM	Kitchener	Conestoga College
CFRC-FM	101.9 FM	Kingston	Queen's University
CIXX-FM	106.9 FM	London	Fanshawe College
CHRW-FM	94.9 FM	London	University of Western Ontario
CKDJ-FM	107.9 FM	Ottawa	Algonquin College

CKC455	91.9 FM	Mississauga	University of Toronto Mississauga
CKCU-FM	93.1 FM	Ottawa	Carleton University
CHUO-FM	89.1 FM	Ottawa	University of Ottawa
CFFF-FM †	92.7 FM	Peterborough	Trent University
CFBU-FM	103.7 FM	St. Catharines	Brock University
CKLU-FM	96.7 FM	Sudbury	Laurentian University
CILU-FM	102.7 FM	Thunder Bay	Lakehead University
CJRU	1280 AM	Toronto	Ryerson University
CKHC-FM	96.9 FM	Toronto	Humber College
CIUT-FM	89.5 FM	Toronto	University of Toronto
CHRY-FM	105.5 FM	Toronto	York University
CKMS-FM †	102.7 FM	Waterloo	University of Waterloo
CRNC	90.1 FM (cable only)	Welland	Niagara College
CJAM-FM	99.1 FM	Windsor	University of Windsor
Quebec			
CJLO	1690 AM	Montreal	Concordia University

CKUT-FM	90.3 FM	Montreal	McGill University
CISM-FM	89.3 FM	Montreal	Université de Montréal
CHYZ-FM	94.3 FM	Quebec City	Université Laval
CJMQ-FM †	88.9 FM	Sherbrooke	Bishop's University
CFAK-FM	88.3 FM	Sherbrooke	Université de Sherbrooke
CFOU-FM	89.1 FM	Trois-Rivières	Université du Québec à Trois-Rivières

But even more handy, you can find a list of contact information for every single college radio station through the NCRA: https://www.ncra.ca/members/member-directory. The NCRA used to have this wicked program where you could pay $40 and send out 40 CDS to every single campus radio station. It was amazing. I tried to do it about 5 years ago and the new Marketing Manager had never heard of it. Ask your college campus if they are still running it. If not - use this list as a resource, and send out 40 copies of your CDS, whether physically through the mail, or by contacting Station Managers directly.

Campus radio is the first step to commercial airplay. You need to be charting somewhere. Your goal is not to get to the top of your local campus's charts, but to chart on the Top 20 for your genre, and eventually get into the Top 100 for the month. Ask for interviews wherever possible, ask to schedule live to airs or even Instagram takeovers. This is an incredibly underused resource.

Howdy, you've reached the end

So here we are. Why did I make you watch a cow dancing, on endless repeat, for 10 hours? Well, you see, being an excellent musician is simply not enough in the age of social media. You must be entertaining as well. When users find value in the content, aka, the substance of what you're writing, it becomes a lot easier to sell them on whatever idea or facet you're trying to market. It matters that you're marketable on top of having incredible musicianship & talent.

Don't waste your time if you haven't sunk just as much time into your craft. There are many smart marketers that have become viral sensations, but that doesn't last if you don't have material and plan to continue going.

Always be entertaining. Remember - our roles as artists/musicians are to entertain - to bring happiness and light to one another, and to remind people of the moments in life that make us feel emotions. This isn't the same for everyone. This can mean that you're only pulling on emotional muses and difficult moments in your life. This can mean you're simply reminding your fans of the regular upbeat moments of life. It can be anywhere in between. But most importantly, you're filling your role to entertain your audience, and to keep them engaged. There is a reason that stupid video has 23 million views. Think about that for a moment. Being entertaining is very important. It's up to you to find the mix between substance and entertainment.